WHAT A WORLD 1
READING
SECOND EDITION

Amazing Stories
from Around the Globe

D0140672

Milada Broukal

PEARSON
Longman

What a World Reading 1: Amazing Stories from Around the Globe

Pearson Education, 10 Bank Street, White Plains, NY 10606

Staff credits: The people who made up the *What a World Reading 1* team, representing editorial, production, design, and manufacturing, are Pietro Alongi, Rhea Banker, John Brezinsky, Aerin Csigay, Nancy Flaggman, Françoise Leffler, Amy McCormick, Linda Moser, Robert Ruvo, Jennifer Stem, Katherine Sullivan, Paula Van Ells, and Patricia Wosczyk.
Cover and text design: Patricia Wosczyk
Text composition: ElectraGraphics, Inc.
Text font: Minion
Photo Credits: Cover, Christian Kober/Robert Harding World Imagery/Corbis; Page 1, Jeremy Sutton-Hibbert/Alamy; p. 7, Kord.com/age fotostock/Imagestate; p. 14, Julian Love/Photolibrary; p. 20, Shutterstock.com; p. 26, Mohammed Ansar/Photolibrary; p. 32, (fish) Shutterstock.com; p. 32, (background) double A/Shutterstock p. 38, Sabine Lubenow/Photolibrary; p. 44, Jacques Jangoux/Photolibrary; p. 50, Shutterstock.com; p. 56, Corbis/Photolibrary; p. 68, Hulton-Deutsch Collection/Corbis; p. 74, Steve Bloom Images/Alamy; p. 80, Robert Harding World Imagery/Getty Images; p. 86, Shutterstock.com; p. 92, Shutterstock.com; p. 98, Reuters/Corbis; p. 104, Dreamstime.com; p. 111, David South/Alamy; p. 117, Stefano Bianchetti/Corbis; p. 123, AP Images/Tom Hood.

Library of Congress Cataloging-in-Publication Data

Broukal, Milada.
  What a world reading: amazing stories from around the globe / Milada Broukal.—2nd ed.
    p. cm—(What a world reading: amazing stories from around the globe series)
  Includes index.
  Previous ed.: 2004.
  ISBN 0-13-247267-8 (v. 1)—ISBN 0-13-247796-3 (v. 2)—ISBN 0-13-138201-2 (v. 3) 1. English language—Textbooks for foreign speakers. 2. Readers—Manners and customs.
  PE1128.B7165 2010
  428.6'4—dc22

2010020089

ISBN-13: 978-0-13-247267-8
ISBN-10: 0-13-247267-8

PEARSON LONGMAN ON THE WEB

Pearsonlongman.com offers online resources for teachers and students. Access our Companion Websites, our online catalog, and our local offices around the world.

Visit us at **www.pearsonlongman.com**.

Printed in the United States of America
1 2 3 4 5 6 7 8 9 10—V011—19 18 17 16 15 14 13 12 11 10

CONTENTS

INTRODUCTION

What a World: Amazing Stories from Around the Globe—the series

This series now has two strands: a reading strand and a listening strand. Both strands explore linked topics from around the world and across history. They can be used separately or together for maximum exploration of content and development of essential reading and listening skills.

	Reading Strand	Listening Strand
Level 1 (Beginning)	*What a World Reading 1, 2e*	*What a World Listening 1*
Level 2 (High-Beginning)	*What a World Reading 2, 2e*	*What a World Listening 2*
Level 3 (Intermediate)	*What a World Reading 3, 2e*	*What a World Listening 3*

What a World Reading 1, 2e—a beginning reader

It is the first in a three-book series of readings for English language learners. The twenty units in this book correspond thematically with the units in *What a World Listening 1*. Each topic is about a different person, society, animal, place, custom, or organization. The topics span history and the globe, from the Sami of northern Europe, to the Great Wall of China, to life in Antarctica.

New to the Second Edition

- New and updated readings: there are eight new readings
- Critical thinking questions have been added in every unit to develop students' thinking skills
- Internet activities have been added for every unit to build students' Internet research skills; these activities are in the Appendices at the back of the book

Unit Structure and Approach

BEFORE YOU READ opens with a picture of the person, society, animal, place, custom, or organization featured in the unit. Prereading questions follow. Their purpose is to motivate students to read, encourage predictions about the content of the reading, and involve the students' own experiences when possible. Vocabulary can be presented as the need arises.

READING passages should be first done individually by skimming for the general content. The teacher may wish to explain the bolded vocabulary words at this point. The students should then do a second, closer reading. Further reading(s) can be done aloud.

VOCABULARY exercises focus on the boldfaced words in the reading. There are three types of vocabulary exercises. Both *Meaning* and *Words That Go Together* are definition exercises that encourage students to work out the meanings of words from the context. *Meaning* focuses on single words. *Words That Go Together* focuses on collocations or groups of words which are easier to learn together the way they are used in the language. The third exercise, *Use*, reinforces the vocabulary further by making students use the words or collocations in a meaningful, yet possibly different, context. This section can be done during or after the reading phase, or both.

COMPREHENSION exercises appear in each unit and consist of *Understanding the Reading* and *Remembering Details*. These are followed by either *Understanding the Sequence* or *Sentence Completion*. All confirm the content of the text either in general or in detail. These exercises for developing reading skills can be done individually, in pairs, in small groups, or as a class. It is preferable to do these exercises in conjunction with the text, since they are not meant to test memory. The comprehension exercises end with *Tell the Story* or *Dictation* which are speaking activities.

DISCUSSION questions encourage students to bring their own ideas and imagination to the related topics in each reading. They can also provide insights into cultural similarities and differences.

CRITICAL THINKING questions give students the opportunity to develop thinking skills (comparing and contrasting cultural customs, recognizing personal attitudes and values, etc.)

WRITING exercises provide the stimulus for students to write simple sentences about the reading. Teachers should use their own discretion when deciding whether or not to correct the writing exercises.

SPELLING AND PUNCTUATION exercises provide basic rules and accompanying activities for spelling or punctuation, using examples from the readings.

Additional Activities

INTERNET ACTIVITIES (in the Appendices) give students the opportunity to develop their Internet research skills. Each activity can be done in a classroom setting or if the students have Internet Access, as homework leading to a presentation or discussion in class. There is an Internet activity for each unit and it is always related to the theme of the unit. It helps students evaluate websites for their reliability and gets them to process and put together the information in an organized way.

SELF-TESTS after Unit 10 and Unit 20 review comprehension, sentence structure, vocabulary, and spelling and punctuation in a multiple-choice format.

$$* * * * *$$

The **Answer Key** for *What a World Reading 1, 2e* is available at the following website: http://www.pearsonlongman.com/whataworld.

UNIT 1

WHO IS J. K. ROWLING?

you read

before

Answer these questions.

1. What do you know about *Harry Potter*?
2. Is Harry Potter a real person?
3. How many *Harry Potter* books are there?

WHO IS J. K. ROWLING?

1   J. K. Rowling is the **author** of the *Harry Potter* books. J. K.'s name is Joanne Kathleen. She was born in 1965 in a small town near Bristol, England. Joanne lived with her parents and her sister. The Rowling family was not rich. Joanne did not go to **special** schools. She was a **quiet** child. She loved to read and write stories. Joanne went to Exeter University, and she graduated in 1987. After graduation, she moved to London where she worked at different office jobs. In her **free time**, she wrote stories.

2   In 1990, Joanne's mother died. Joanne was sad, and she wanted to leave England. She saw an ad in the newspaper for a job as an English teacher. The job was in Portugal. She had an **interview**, and she got the job. In Portugal, Joanne married a Portuguese man. The next year, Joanne had a daughter, but she was not happy in her marriage. She left Portugal with her daughter and went to live in Edinburgh, Scotland, near her sister.

3   Life was very difficult for Joanne. She **took care of** her daughter. She was **alone**, and nobody helped her. She had no money and no job. Then one day, on a train, she thought about the *Harry Potter* story. She began to write that story. Joanne liked to go to a coffee shop to write. She sat there for many hours. She drank coffee and wrote. Her daughter slept beside her.

4   After five years, Joanne finished writing the first *Harry Potter* book. She sent it to many book publishers. They all said that they didn't like it. Finally, a publisher liked it, but the publisher said, "This is a children's book. **Adults** won't read it. You won't **make** a lot of **money**." In 1997, Joanne's dream to publish her book **came true**: *Harry Potter and the Sorcerer's Stone* was in the bookstores. Children and their parents loved the book, and it became famous **all over the world**.

5   Now *Harry Potter* is in sixty-five languages. The publisher was wrong about one thing: Everyone loves *Harry Potter*—children and adults. Over 100 million books were sold in 1999. Then two *Harry Potter* books became popular movies. J. K. Rowling wrote four more *Harry Potter* books after that. All those books became movies, too! On January 11, 2007, J. K. Rowling finished her seventh and last *Harry Potter* book. She will continue to write, but not *Harry Potter* books. The question is, what will people do without *Harry Potter*?

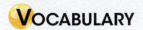VOCABULARY

MEANING

Write the correct words in the blanks.

adults	author	quiet
alone	interview	special

1. J. K. Rowling is a(n) _____. She writes books.

2. Joanne was not a noisy child. She was _____.

3. Joanne went to regular, ordinary schools. She did not go to _____ schools.

4. Children like *Harry Potter*. Many _____ like *Harry Potter*, too. People of all ages like *Harry Potter*.

5. Joanne lived _____. She did not live with another person.

6. Joanne had a meeting about a new job. She had an _____.

WORDS THAT GO TOGETHER

Write the correct words in the blanks.

all over the world	free time	took care of
came true	make money	

1. Joanne wrote when she didn't work. She wrote stories in her

   _____.

2. Joanne watched and helped her daughter. Joanne

   _____ her.

3. Joanne writes books, and the book publisher pays her. She will

   _____.

4. *Harry Potter* is famous in every country. It is famous

   _____.

5. Good things happened to Joanne. All of her dreams

   _____.

USE

Work with a partner to answer the questions. Use complete sentences.

1. Who is the *author* of this book?
2. What do you do when you are *alone*?
3. Who is a *quiet* student in your class?
4. What do you do in your *free time*?
5. What fast food is famous *all over the world*?
6. What questions do people ask at an *interview*?

COMPREHENSION

UNDERSTANDING THE READING

Circle the letter of the correct answer.

1. Joanne was _____.

   a. not from a rich family   **b.** from a big family   **c.** a bad child

2. Joanne _____ and went to Portugal.

   a. got a job   **b.** got married   **c.** wrote her book

3. *Harry Potter* is a book for _____.

   a. children   **b.** adults   **c.** children and adults

REMEMBERING DETAILS

*Circle **T** if the sentence is true. Circle **F** if the sentence is false.*

1. Joanne was an English teacher in Portugal.   T   F

2. Joanne married an English man in Portugal.   T   F

3. Joanne left her daughter in Portugal.   T   F

4. Joanne finished writing the first *Harry Potter* book after five years.   T   F

5. Every publisher liked her book.   T   F

6. *Harry Potter* is in forty-two languages.   T   F

UNDERSTANDING THE SEQUENCE

Which happened first? Write **1** on the line. Which happened second? Write **2** on the line.

1. _____ Joanne became an English teacher.

   _____ Joanne worked at different office jobs.

2. _____ Joanne thought about *Harry Potter* on the train.

   _____ Joanne wrote about *Harry Potter* in the coffee shop.

3. _____ Joanne finished *Harry Potter*.

   _____ Joanne sent *Harry Potter* to publishers.

4. _____ Two *Harry Potter* books became movies.

   _____ *Harry Potter* was in the bookstores.

TELL THE STORY

Work with a partner. Tell the story of J. K. Rowling to your partner. Use your own words. Your partner asks you questions about the story. Then your partner tells you the story and you ask questions.

DISCUSSION

Discuss the answers to these questions with your classmates.

1. Why is *Harry Potter* so popular?
2. The *Harry Potter* story is not real. Do you like to read stories that are real or not real? Why?
3. Adults and children like *Harry Potter*. What are other books or movies that adults and children like?

CRITICAL THINKING

Work with a partner. Ask each other the following questions. Discuss your answers.

1. To *inspire* someone means "to give them courage to act." The story of J. K. Rowling inspires many people. What does she inspire people to do? Does she inspire you? Why or why not?
2. From an early age, J. K. Rowling wanted to be a writer. If you could be whatever you wanted, what would it be? Why? Would you like to be famous? Why or why not?

WRITING

Complete the sentences about J. K. Rowling.

EXAMPLE   J. K. Rowling is _an author_ _____.

1. J. K. Rowling wrote_____.

2. Joanne is from _____.

3. Joanne worked _____.

4. Joanne married _____.

5. *Harry Potter* is _____.

SPELLING AND PUNCTUATION

CAPITAL LETTERS: NAMES, PLACES, NATIONALITIES, AND LANGUAGES

We use a **capital letter** for:

- **People's names** and **initials**
  *Joanne Rowling and **J. K.** Rowling are the same person.*

- Names of **cities**, **states**, **countries**, and **continents**
  London   Florida   Portugal   Africa

- **Nationalities** and **languages**
  Americans love her books. You can read her books in Spanish, French, and German.

Underline the words that need capital letters. Write the correct words on the lines.

1. The name of the boy is harry potter.   _____

2. Joanne rowling lived in edinburgh.   _____

3. You can read *harry potter* in spanish.   _____

4. She didn't go to spain, but she went to portugal.   _____

5. She married a portuguese man.   _____

6. She lived near bristol in england.   _____

 *Go to page 135 for the Internet Activity.*

WHAT ARE SOME NEW YEAR'S CUSTOMS?

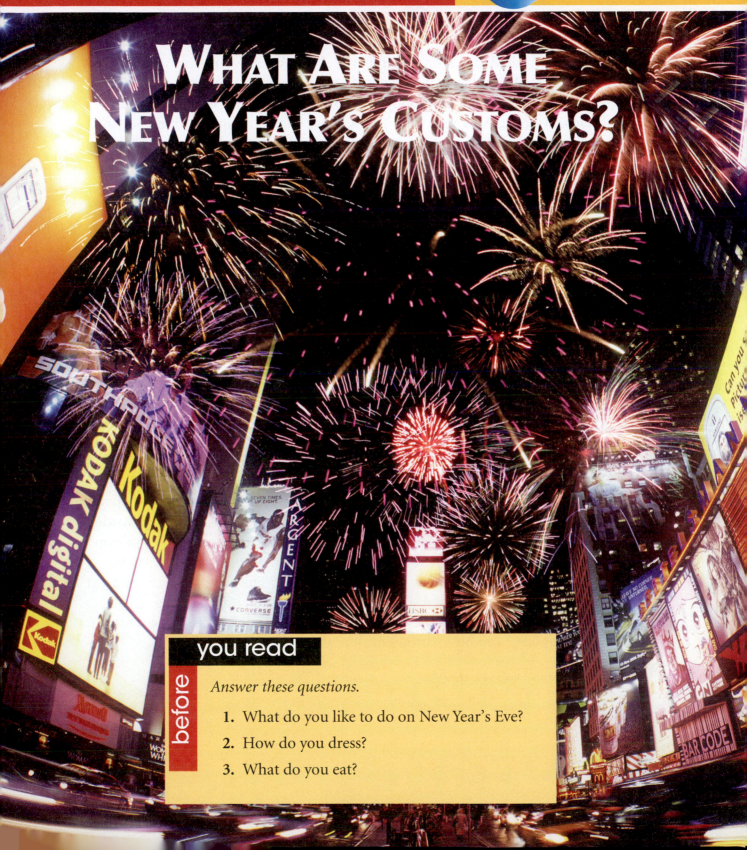

you read

before

Answer these questions.

1. What do you like to do on New Year's Eve?
2. How do you dress?
3. What do you eat?

WHAT ARE SOME NEW YEAR'S CUSTOMS?

1   In the United States, on December 31, New Year's Eve, people wait for the clock to **strike** midnight. Some people go to parties, and others stay at home. Just before midnight, everybody turns on their television sets to watch the **celebrations** in New York City. There, above a tall building in Times Square, a big crystal ball drops **at the stroke of** midnight. People kiss and say, "Happy New Year!" Then there are **fireworks** to welcome the New Year.

2   Some Americans also follow old **traditions** to bring them **wealth** in the New Year. In some parts of the United States, people eat black-eyed peas,[1] greens, and corn bread[2] to bring them wealth. Black-eyed peas look like money, greens are the color of dollars, and corn bread is the color of gold. People all over the world have traditions to bring wealth in the New Year.

3   People wear certain clothes and eat certain foods on New Year's Eve or New Year's Day. For example, in the Philippines, people wear clothes with circles on them or polka dots. Circles look like money and people hope money will come to them. They also eat round fruits and throw **coins** at the stroke of midnight to be rich that year. In parts of South America, people wear yellow underwear on New Year's Eve to bring them wealth. In Brazil, they eat lentils on New Year's Day because lentils look like money. In Spanish-speaking countries, people eat twelve **grapes** at midnight on New Year's Eve. They eat one grape for each stroke of the clock until it is midnight. In the Netherlands, people eat round doughnuts called *Olie Bollen* or "oil balls" to bring wealth.

4   In Scotland, there is an old tradition called *First Footing*. For good luck in the New Year, a tall, dark, handsome man must be the first person to **step inside** your home after midnight. To make it easy, people often make such a person stand outside the home before midnight. Just as the clock strikes 12:00, the person walks into the home. He is the first visitor. The visitor must have a gift in his hand, too. A gift of a silver or gold coin is good. It **represents** wealth coming into the home all through the year. Be careful! The first footer must not have flat feet,[3] and his eyebrows must not meet **in the middle**!

---

[1] **black-eyed peas**: dried white beans with a black "eye" on them
[2] **corn bread**: a cakelike bread made with corn
[3] **flat feet**: feet without a curve in the middle

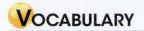

VOCABULARY

MEANING

Write the correct words in the blanks.

celebrations	fireworks	represents	traditions
coins	grapes	strike	wealth

1. On New Year's Eve, people wait for the clock to _____ midnight.

2. At midnight, there are New Year _____ everywhere.

3. You hear bangs, and then the sky is full of _____.

4. People do these things every year for many years. These are _____ for them.

5. People eat special foods to bring them _____ in the New Year.

6. Some people throw _____ or metal money.

7. In Spanish-speaking countries, at midnight on New Year's Eve, people eat twelve _____. These are small round fruits that people use for making wine.

8. In Scotland, a gift of gold or silver that comes in after midnight in the New Year _____ wealth, or means that money will come in the New Year.

WORDS THAT GO TOGETHER

Write the correct words in the blanks.

at the stroke of	in the middle	step inside

1. Some people have eyebrows that join or meet _____.

2. In Times Square, the crystal ball drops _____ midnight.

3. A tall, dark, handsome man must be the first to _____ your home after midnight.

USE

Work with a partner to answer the questions. Use complete sentences.

1. What is one of your favorite family *traditions*?
2. What can you make from *grapes*?
3. How many *coins* do you have on you?
4. When are there *fireworks* in your town or city?
5. What is something people buy to show their *wealth*?
6. What thing or number *represents* good luck to you?

COMPREHENSION

UNDERSTANDING THE READING

Circle the letter of the correct answer.

1. On New Year's Eve, people _____.

    a. pray for wealth

    b. usually stay at home

    c. follow many different traditions

2. To bring wealth in the New Year, people _____.

    a. go to parties or watch television

    b. eat certain foods and wear special clothes

    c. throw round fruits and coins outside

3. In Scotland, to bring good luck in the New Year, a tall, dark, handsome man must

    _____.

    a. give away silver and gold coins to everyone he meets

    b. be the first visitor to a house on New Year's Day

    c. step outside the house as the clock strikes midnight

REMEMBERING DETAILS

Circle **T** *if the sentence is true. Circle* **F** *if the sentence is false.*

1. On New Year's Eve, Americans usually watch the celebrations in Times Square.   T   F

2. Some Americans eat black-eyed peas to bring them wealth in the New Year.   T   F

3. In the Philippines, people wear clothes with polka dots on New Year's Day.   T   F

4. Brazilians eat grapes on New Year's Day.   T   F

5. The Scots have a New Year tradition called *First Stepping*.   T   F

6. In this tradition, a handsome man with flat feet brings luck to   T   F
   a home in the New Year if he walks in the door after midnight.

SENTENCE COMPLETION

Match the words in column A and column B to make sentences.

	A		B
_____ 1.	Americans may go to	a.	and say, "Happy New Year!"
_____ 2.	At home, many Americans	b.	parties or stay at home.
_____ 3.	Some Americans go	c.	watch television.
_____ 4.	People kiss	d.	to Times Square in New York.
_____ 5.	They watch	e.	to welcome the New Year.
_____ 6.	There are fireworks	f.	a big crystal ball drop at midnight.

DICTATION

Work with a partner. Read three sentences from the exercise above. Your partner listens and writes the sentences. Then your partner reads three sentences and you write them.

DISCUSSION

Discuss the answers to these questions with your classmates.

1. When do you celebrate the New Year in your country? What are the New Year's customs? What do they mean?

2. Do you like to celebrate the New Year? Why or why not? Do you make New Year's resolutions (promises)?

3. Do you hope for wealth in the New Year? Why or why not? Do you think people should hope for wealth or for something else? What do you usually want for the New Year?

CRITICAL THINKING

Work with a partner. Ask each other the following questions. Discuss your answers.

1. Some people believe that eating black-eyed peas or wearing clothes with polka dots can bring a person wealth. Where do you think traditions like these came from? Why do people still follow them? Do you believe in any traditions that bring luck or wealth? Why or why not?

2. Why do you think that people all over the world celebrate the New Year? Why is it important? What does it mean to people?

WRITING

Complete the sentences about your New Year's Day.

EXAMPLE   In my country, New Year's Day is on *January 1*_____.

1. On New Year's Day, I wear _____.

2. On New Year's Day, we eat _____.

3. On New Year's Day, people don't _____.

4. On New Year's Day, I like to _____.

5. On New Year's Day, I don't like to _____.

SPELLING AND PUNCTUATION

CAPITAL LETTERS: DAYS, MONTHS, AND HOLIDAYS

We use a **capital letter** for:

- Names of **days**
  Sunday   *Monday*   *Friday*

- Names of **months**
  January   *March*   *December*

- Names of **holidays**
  Thanksgiving   *Christmas*   *New Year's Day*

We do **NOT** use capital letters for the names of **seasons**.
  spring   *summer*   *autumn (fall)*   *winter*

A. *Underline the words that need capital letters. Remember the capital letter rules from Unit 1.*

1. In brazil, people eat lentils on new year's day.

2. In south america, new year's day is in the summer.

3. The chinese new year comes between january 21 and february 19.

4. The iranians celebrate new year's day in the spring.

5. Americans celebrate thanksgiving on the last thursday in november.

B. *Answer the questions. Use correct capital letters.*

1. What is your favorite holiday? _____

2. In what month is your favorite holiday? _____

3. On what day of the week is this holiday this year? _____

 Go to page 135 for the Internet Activity.

DID YOU KNOW?	**In Japan:** • New Year's Day is the most important holiday and is celebrated from January 1–3. • It is a tradition to go to the temple or shrine on New Year's Day. • Homes and entrances are decorated for the New Year with pine, bamboo, and plum trees.	

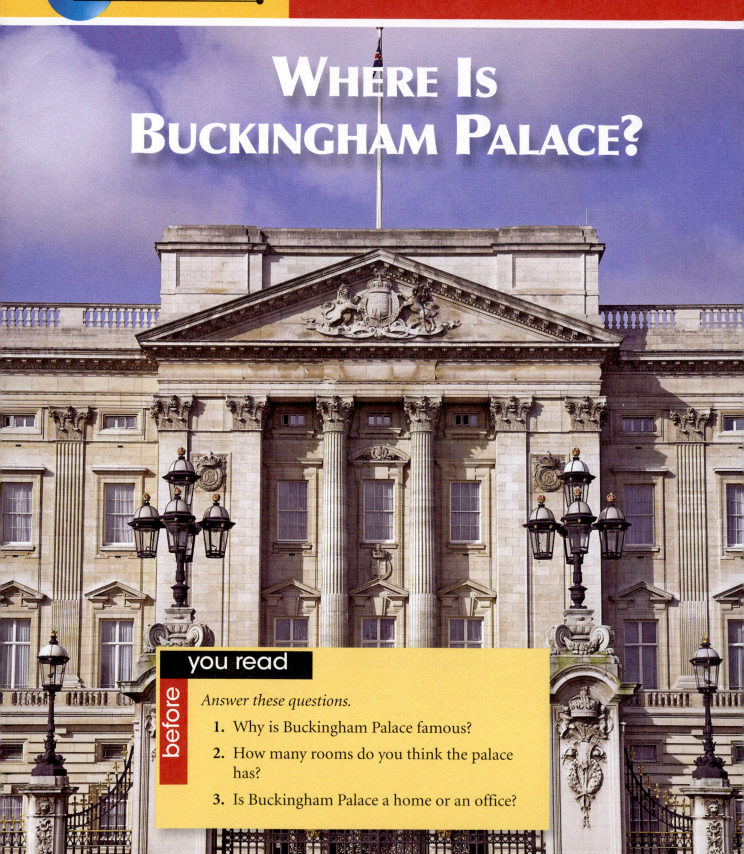

WHERE IS BUCKINGHAM PALACE?

you read

before

Answer these questions.

1. Why is Buckingham Palace famous?

2. How many rooms do you think the palace has?

3. Is Buckingham Palace a home or an office?

WHERE IS BUCKINGHAM PALACE?

1   Buckingham Palace is in London, England. Buckingham Palace was built around 1705. It is famous because Queen Elizabeth of England lives there. She became queen in 1952.

2   Buckingham Palace is a big and beautiful building. A **flag** flies over the palace. It flies **on top of** the palace when the queen is there. Queen Elizabeth and her family live on the second **floor** of the palace. The queen also has her office at the palace. Presidents, kings, and **politicians** meet with her. Queen Elizabeth often asks important people to eat dinner at the palace. She also has three **garden** parties in the summer. She invites 9,000 people to each party! **A lot of** people meet the queen.

3   Buckingham Palace is like a small town. It has a police station, a hospital, two post offices, a movie theater, a swimming pool, two sports clubs, a garden, and a lake. The palace has about 600 rooms. Almost 400 people work there. Two of them have very unusual jobs. They take care of the clocks. There are 300 clocks in Buckingham Palace!

4   Queen Elizabeth's day starts at 7:00 in the morning. Seven people take care of her. One person **prepares** her bath, and another person prepares her clothes. Another person takes care of her dogs. The queen loves dogs. Right now, she has eight dogs. Every day, a man brings food for the dogs to Queen Elizabeth's room. The queen puts the food in the **bowls** with a silver spoon.

5   At 8:30 every morning, the queen has breakfast with her husband, Prince Philip. They drink a special coffee with hot milk. During breakfast, a musician plays Scottish music outside. Then Queen Elizabeth works in her office **the rest of** the morning. After lunch, she visits hospitals, schools, or new buildings.

6   It is very interesting to eat dinner at Buckingham Palace. You have to **follow rules**. Queen Elizabeth starts to eat first, and then everybody eats. When the queen finishes eating, everybody finishes eating. You can't leave the table during dinner. The queen never accepts a telephone call during dinner, even in an **emergency**.

7   Parts of Buckingham Palace are open to visitors in August and September. What visitors see are the "state rooms" where the queen usually entertains presidents and kings. But, visitors, don't think you are going to see the queen . . . In August and September, Her Majesty is on vacation.

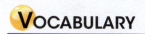

VOCABULARY

MEANING

Write the correct words in the blanks.

bowls	flag	garden	prepares
emergency	floor	politicians	

1. Buckingham Palace has a large _____ with a great variety of flowers and plants.

2. The queen doesn't get her clothes ready. A person _____ the queen's clothes for her.

3. The prime minister and the president are important _____. They are the leaders of their country's government.

4. England's _____ flies on top of the palace.

5. The queen lives on the second _____ of the palace.

6. The queen sometimes gets a very important telephone call. Sometimes the call is an _____.

7. The queen puts the dogs' food in round dishes. She puts it in _____.

WORDS THAT GO TOGETHER

Write the correct words in the blanks.

a lot of	follow rules	on top of	the rest of

1. The queen works in her office for one part of the day. Then she goes to other places for _____ the day.

2. Many people meet the queen. _____ people go to her garden parties.

3. There is a flag _____ Buckingham Palace. It is the highest part of the palace.

4. At dinner with the queen, you must _____. There are some things you are allowed to do and other things you are not allowed to do.

USE

Work with a partner to answer the questions. Use complete sentences.

1. What do you put in *bowls*?
2. What do you see *a lot of* on the street?
3. What are the colors of your country's *flag*?
4. What *floor* is your classroom on?
5. Who *prepares* dinner in your home?
6. Who is a famous *politician*?
7. When there is an *emergency*, like a fire, what do you do?

COMPREHENSION

UNDERSTANDING THE READING

Circle the letter of the correct answer.

1. Buckingham Palace is _____.

    a. near a small town   **b.** a new building   **c.** the home of the queen

2. Buckingham Palace is _____.

    a. like a town   **b.** famous for its flag   **c.** a very small palace

3. You can visit some of the rooms in Buckingham Palace _____.

    a. all year   **b.** in August and September   **c.** when the queen is there

REMEMBERING DETAILS

Reread the passage and answer the questions.

1. Where is Buckingham Palace?
2. What floor does the queen live on?
3. When does the queen have garden parties?
4. How many people does she invite?
5. How many rooms does the palace have?
6. When does the queen start her day?
7. What does the queen do after lunch?

SENTENCE COMPLETION

Match the words in column A and column B to make sentences.

	A		B
_____ 1.	The queen visits	a.	the telephone during dinner.
_____ 2.	The queen has breakfast	b.	hospitals, schools, or new buildings.
_____ 3.	The queen never answers	c.	in her office in the morning.
_____ 4.	The queen works	d.	at 8:30 in the morning.
_____ 5.	People can visit	e.	a lot of people.
_____ 6.	The queen meets	f.	some rooms of the palace in August and September.

DICTATION

Work with a partner. Read three sentences from the exercise above. Your partner listens and writes the sentences. Then your partner reads three sentences and you write them.

DISCUSSION

Discuss the answers to these questions with your classmates.

1. Do you think the queen has a wonderful life? Give reasons.
2. Do countries need kings and queens?
3. What other countries have kings or queens? What are these kings and queens like? What do they do?

CRITICAL THINKING

Work with a partner. Ask each other the following questions. Discuss your answers.

1. Would you like to live in a palace? Why or why not? If you could live any way you liked, how and where would you live? Imagine a day there. What is your day like from morning until night?
2. Do you think wealth and palaces bring happiness? Why or why not? What are the most important things that bring happiness in life? What small things make you happy in your everyday life?

WRITING

Complete the sentences about Buckingham Palace and the queen.

EXAMPLE   The queen lives _in Buckingham Palace_____.

1. Buckingham Palace was built _____.

2. Buckingham Palace is _____.

3. Buckingham Palace has _____.

4. The queen has breakfast _____.

5. After lunch, the queen visits _____.

SPELLING AND PUNCTUATION

WORDS WITH *QU*

> We spell the /**kw**/ sound *qu* in most English words. Never use *q* alone.
> Always use *qu*. A vowel (*a, e, i, o*) always follows *qu*.
>
> *qu*ality   *qu*ick   e*qu*al   s*qu*irrel
> *qu*een   *qu*ote   ban*qu*et

Underline the misspelled words. Write the correct words on the lines.

1. The qween lives in the palace.   _____

2. It is qiet in the palace.   _____

3. She gives many banqwets.   _____

4. You must never skweeze her hand.   _____

5. Guests eat kwality food.   _____

6. She doesn't eat qwuickly.   _____

7. A guest never asks her a qwestion.   _____

🖱 *Go to page 135 for the Internet Activity.*

DID YOU KNOW?

- All the windows in Buckingham Palace are cleaned every six weeks.
- During World War II, the palace had nine bomb hits. Only one person died.

Where Is Buckingham Palace?   **19**

UNIT 4

WHY ARE COWS SPECIAL IN INDIA?

before you read

Answer these questions.

1. What do you know about cows?

2. Look at the picture. Why are the cows in the street?

3. Where do you see cows in your country?

WHY ARE COWS SPECIAL IN INDIA?

1   About 1 billion people live in India. Many people live on small **farms**. They live a quiet and simple life. The family takes care of the farm and the animals. The most important animal on the farm is the cow. The cow helps on the farm in two ways. It gives milk to the family, and it works on the farm.

2   The farmers don't make a lot of money. They can't buy machines to help them do their work. Also, the weather is a **problem** in India. In June, July, August, and September, there's a lot of rain. The **ground** gets very wet. Then the ground gets **soft**. A machine cannot work on soft ground, but a cow can. Cows also do not **cost** a lot of money. They don't need gasoline or **repairs** like machines.

3   Farmers care about their cows very much. They want their cows to be happy. The farms aren't busy at certain times of the year. At these times, people wash their cows. Americans like to wash their cars, and Indians like to wash their cows! In addition, two times a year, there are special religious[1] celebrations for the cows. Then the farmers **decorate** their cows and take them to a Hindu temple.[2] Most people in India are Hindus. In the Hindu religion, the gods[3] **protect** the cows. The cows are sacred animals. Hindus have to take good care of cows and protect them. They cannot kill cows.

4   The cows are also protected by the government. In India, it's **against the law** to kill a cow. So when cows get too old to work, farmers send their old cows away from the farm. The cows walk around free in the streets. People give them food, and drivers are careful not to **hit** them. There are also special animal hospitals for old or sick cows. The government and some rich people give money to these hospitals.

5   People in other countries do not understand why the Indian government **spends money on** cows. There are many poor people in India who need money. Indians say that Americans spend more money on cats and dogs. People in India care for over 200 million cows every year. They have cared for cows **for a long time**. It's a tradition that is thousands of years old.

---

[1] **religious:** related to religion (belief in one or more gods)
[2] **temple**: a building where people in some religions go to pray to their gods
[3] **gods**: beings believed to control the world

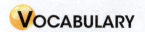

MEANING

Write the correct words in the blanks.

cost	farms	hit	protect	soft
decorate	ground	problem	repairs	

1. Cows live on land where people grow food and keep animals. They live on

    _____.

2. The land we walk on is called the _____.

3. The ground is _____. It is not hard.

4. Cows do not _____ a lot of money. They have a low price.

5. The car doesn't work. It needs _____.

6. In July, it rains a lot. It is bad for the land. The rain is a _____.

7. Drivers do not want to _____ the cows. They do not want to hurt
    the cows.

8. People put things on their cows. They want the cows to look nice. They

    _____ the cows.

9. In the Hindu religion, cows are sacred animals. Hindus have to

    _____ the cows. They have to keep them safe.

WORDS THAT GO TOGETHER

Write the correct words in the blanks.

against the law	for a long time	spends money on

1. People are not allowed to kill cows in India. It is _____.

2. In India, the government _____ its cows. The government
    pays for many things for the cows.

3. Indians have loved cows for thousands of years. They have cared about them

    _____.

USE

Work with a partner to answer the questions. Use complete sentences.

1. What do you *spend* a lot of *money on*?
2. What is *against the law* in your country?
3. What is something that is *soft*?
4. What animals do you see on *farms*?
5. What *repairs* do you make in your home?
6. What is a *problem* you have in English?

COMPREHENSION

UNDERSTANDING THE READING

Circle the letter of the correct answer.

1. Cows help farmers because cows _____.

   a. work on farms   **b.** walk around the streets   **c.** eat grass

2. In India, people do not _____.

   a. kill cows   **b.** take care of cows   **c.** have hospitals for cows

3. In India, the government spends money on _____.

   a. cats   **b.** dogs   **c.** cows

REMEMBERING DETAILS

*Circle **T** if the sentence is true. Circle **F** if the sentence is false.*

1. In India, there is one celebration for the cows every year.   T   F
2. Indians take care of 20 million cows every year.   T   F
3. Drivers are careful not to hit the cows.   T   F
4. Indians wash and decorate their cows every day.   T   F
5. Indians spend money on cats and dogs.   T   F
6. Farmers want their cows to be happy.   T   F

SENTENCE COMPLETION

Match the words in column A and column B to make sentences.

	A			B
_____	**1.** Indians want		**a.**	free in the streets.
_____	**2.** The government pays for		**b.**	their cows to be happy.
_____	**3.** An old cow walks		**c.**	special animal hospitals.
_____	**4.** Cows give milk and		**d.**	after it rains.
_____	**5.** Farmers don't have		**e.**	work on small farms.
_____	**6.** Machines cannot work		**f.**	money to buy machines.

DICTATION

Work with a partner. Read three sentences from the exercise above. Your partner listens and writes the sentences. Then your partner reads three sentences and you write them.

DISCUSSION

Discuss the answers to these questions with your classmates.

1. The Indian government spends a lot of money on cows. Is this a good idea? Explain.
2. What animal has a special meaning in your country?
3. The cow celebration is special in India. What is a special celebration in your country?

CRITICAL THINKING

Work with a partner. Ask each other the following questions. Discuss your answers.

1. In the United States, people spend large amounts of money to pay animal doctors when their pets get sick or hurt. Why do you think they do this? Do you think it is a good thing or is it foolish? Why? Do you have a pet? Why or why not?
2. Vegetarians are people who do not eat meat. Some believe it is better for their health. Most believe it is wrong to kill animals for food. Do you think it is wrong to kill animals for food? Why or why not? What are other reasons why people kill animals? Do you think animals should be protected from humans sometimes?

WRITING

Complete the sentences about cows.

EXAMPLE   Cows work *on farms*_____.

1. Cows give _____.

2. Farmers use cows _____.

3. In India, people cannot _____.

4. People in other countries do not understand _____.

5. People in India have cared for _____.

SPELLING AND PUNCTUATION

APOSTROPHES: CONTRACTIONS

> We use an **apostrophe** (') in a contraction. **Contractions** are words with missing letters. We use the apostrophe in place of the missing letters.
> *There is a lot of rain. = There's a lot of rain.*
> *The farms are not busy. = The farms aren't busy.*

Underline the words that need apostrophes for contractions. Write the correct contractions on the lines. One sentence has two contractions.

1. Farmers do not make a lot of money.   _____

2. They cannot buy machines.   _____

3. The ground is not hard.   _____

4. In India, they are careful not to hit cows.   _____

5. There is a cow hospital in the town.   _____

6. It is a tradition that is thousands of years old. _____

Go to page 136 for the Internet Activity.

Go to page 136 for the Internet Activity.

DID YOU KNOW?	• In India, cow's urine is used in many medicines to cure headaches, colds, coughs, and even cancer. • Cow dung is used to make bath soap. • The Sanskrit (ancient language of India) word for "war" means *desire for more cows*.	

WHY DO PEOPLE GIVE GIFTS FOR WEDDINGS?

before

you read

Answer these questions.

1. What kinds of gifts do people give at weddings in your country?

2. What do the parents of the woman give?

3. What do the parents of the man give?

WHY DO PEOPLE GIVE GIFTS FOR WEDDINGS?

1   People give gifts for weddings for different **reasons**. Usually, people want to help the **bride** and **groom**. Many countries have their own customs. In the United States, both families give gifts to the **couple**. In other places, the customs are very different.

2   In India, the groom's family **asks for** a large payment from the bride's family. The payment is called a *dowry*. Sometimes the payment is a special gift with a **brand name**. For example, some families ask for a Singer sewing machine or a Sony television set. Sometimes the payment is money. The money may be **equal to** the family's **income** for two or three years. Both families **agree** about the money. They agree on how much money the bride's family **can afford to** pay. Some Indian families do not like to have many daughters. It is too **expensive**!

3   In the Middle East, the groom gives a gift to his bride. The gift is called a *mahr*. The *mahr* is money and is sometimes land or a home. In Saudi Arabia, the groom gives a lot of money. He buys clothes for the bride for one year and buys furniture for their new home. Rich couples get expensive gifts from both parents. The parents often give nice furniture or a new car.

4   At one time in Saudi Arabia, the *mahr* for a bride was very, very high. Men could not afford to marry Saudi Arabian women. They married women from Lebanon or Egypt. This was bad for Saudi women. Soon, many Saudi women did not have husbands. The government made new rules. They made it hard to marry a **foreigner**. Another Middle Eastern country, Oman, had problems, too. Soldiers in the army could not afford to get married. The sultan of Oman made a law against large *mahr* payments. This helped couples in Oman to get married.

5   A wedding is a very special and important celebration. People give gifts for different reasons, but one thing is the same. Everybody wants to help the bride and groom start a happy life together.

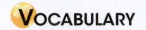

VOCABULARY

MEANING

Write the correct words in the blanks.

agree	couple	foreigner	income
bride	expensive	groom	reasons

1. A man and a woman who are getting married are the _____.

2. The woman who is getting married is the _____.

3. The man who is getting married is the _____.

4. Some families give all the money they get, or their _____, to the groom's family.

5. The man did not marry a woman from his country. He married a _____.

6. Why did the sultan make a new law? What were the _____ why he made the law?

7. The wedding gift was _____. It cost a lot of money.

8. The two families have the same ideas about the wedding gift. They _____ about the wedding gift.

WORDS THAT GO TOGETHER

Write the correct words in the blanks.

asks for	brand name	can afford to	equal to

1. The groom's family wants special things. The family _____ the things they want.

2. Sometimes, a groom asks for money that is the same as or _____ the family's income for a year.

3. The bride's family has enough money for the gift. They _____ buy the gift.

4. People give gifts from famous companies. The gifts they give have a famous _____.

USE

Work with a partner to answer the questions. Use complete sentences.

1. When you go shopping for clothes, what *brand names* do you look for?
2. What color of dress does a *bride* wear in your country?
3. What does a *groom* wear in your country?
4. What does the *couple* do after the wedding ceremony?
5. What are some *reasons* to get married?
6. What problems does a *foreigner* have in a new country?

COMPREHENSION

UNDERSTANDING THE READING

Circle the letter of the correct answer.

1. Wedding-gift customs are _____.

   a. the same all over the world
   b. the same in India and the Middle East
   c. different in most countries

2. In India, the groom's family _____.

   a. gives a large payment
   b. asks for a large payment
   c. asks for furniture

3. In Saudi Arabia, the groom _____.

   a. gives his bride a gift
   b. wants a foreign bride
   c. asks his bride for money

REMEMBERING DETAILS

Circle T if the sentence is true. Circle F if the sentence is false.

1. In the United States, the parents of the bride and groom give gifts.	T	F
2. Indian families like to have many daughters.	T	F
3. In the Middle East, the gift for a bride is called a *mahr*.	T	F
4. At one time, many Saudi women did not have husbands.	T	F
5. The men from Saudi Arabia married women from Oman.	T	F
6. In Oman, the sultan could not afford to get married.	T	F

SENTENCE COMPLETION

Match the words in column A and column B to make sentences.

A	B
_____ 1. Many countries have	a. the couple start a happy life.
_____ 2. Gifts help	b. their own wedding-gift customs.
_____ 3. In the Middle East, the groom	c. very high at one time.
_____ 4. The *mahr* was	d. gives money, land, or a home.
_____ 5. In India, the groom's family	e. a law against large *mahr* payments.
_____ 6. In Oman, the sultan made	f. sometimes asks for gifts with brand names.

DICTATION

Work with a partner. Read three sentences from the exercise above. Your partner listens and writes the sentences. Then your partner reads three sentences and you write them.

DISCUSSION

Discuss the answers to these questions with your classmates.

1. Who pays for weddings in your country?
2. Do you think the custom of giving wedding gifts in your country is good? Why or why not?
3. Some countries have arranged marriages. Do you think this is a good idea?

CRITICAL THINKING

Work with a partner. Ask each other the following questions. Discuss your answers.

1. On what special occasions do people give gifts in your country? Which do you prefer, to give a gift or receive a gift? Why? What does gift-giving do for the giver and the receiver?
2. Why do brides and grooms need help when they marry? What kind of help do young couples need? What are good gifts for them?

WRITING

Complete the sentences about wedding gifts.

EXAMPLE Each country has *its own customs* _____.

1. In the United States, _____.

2. In India, _____.

3. In Saudi Arabia, _____.

4. In Oman, _____.

5. People give gifts _____.

SPELLING AND PUNCTUATION

CAPITAL LETTERS: BRAND NAMES

We use a **capital letter** for the **brand name of a product**.
They like Singer sewing machines.

We do **NOT** use a capital letter for a **product with no special name**.
They use sewing machines to make clothes.

Circle the words that have the correct capitalization for each sentence.

1. The girl's parents are going to buy her a (Dior suit / dior suit).

2. The bride will have a special (wedding dress / Wedding dress).

3. Most people cannot afford to buy a (cartier / Cartier) watch.

4. In most Indian villages, there is a (television / Television) set.

5. The parents gave the couple a (Sony / sony) television.

6. An American (refrigerator / Refrigerator) costs a lot of money in India.

7. The (Electrolux / electrolux) refrigerator is very popular.

Go to page 136 for the Internet Activity.

Go to page 136 for the Internet Activity.

DID YOU KNOW?	• In Thailand, the groom pays the bride's family "sin sod." The amount depends on the social status and education of the bride. A bride who has already been married before does not get "sin sod."	

UNIT 6

WHAT'S SPECIAL ABOUT THE BLOWFISH?

before you read

Answer these questions.

1. Look at the picture. Why would someone eat this fish?

2. Do you know in what country people eat this fish?

3. Do you like to eat fish? Why or why not?

WHAT'S SPECIAL ABOUT THE BLOWFISH?

1   One blowfish has enough **poison** in its small body to kill thirty people. This doesn't stop some people from eating blowfish. In fact, in Japan, people love to eat *fugu* (blowfish) and spend a great deal of money to eat it.

2   The blowfish got this name because it **blows itself up** with water or air into a ball several times its size when it feels **in danger**. There are over 120 kinds of blowfish around the world. Most of them live in warm oceans. They have a smooth skin, but when they blow themselves up, they can have spikes[1] that come out. This is great protection against **enemies**. Of course, their deadly poison is the best protection of all. Most blowfish have bright colors. This tells their enemies they are **dangerous**.

3   Take one **bite** of blowfish and it can kill you. About twenty Japanese people die each year after they eat it. So why do people spend great amounts of money to eat it? It isn't the **flavor** of the fish because it does not have much flavor. It is popular because it is dangerous and because it is the most expensive fish in the world. People eat it to **show off** their courage and their wealth.

4   In Japan, since 1958, only special **chefs** can prepare *fugu* in a restaurant. These chefs train for three years and then take a test. The test is so hard that most chefs do not pass. Japanese law says the chef must show his certificate to the person who is going to eat *fugu*. The chef then prepares the blowfish following strict rules. The poisonous parts go into a special box. The chef must keep careful records of every fish and its parts.

5   The presentation of this special **dish** is very important, too. The chef cuts the meat as thin as paper with a special knife. Then he serves the **raw** fish on a beautiful plate. The **pattern** of the plate, such as a bird or flower, shows through the fish.

6   Some people say they like the taste of blowfish, but others like how it makes them feel. You see, blowfish gives a warm and strange feeling on the lips! There are some people who give money to the chef to leave a certain amount of the poison in because they want all the flavor and feeling! Many chefs will not do this, but some will.

---

[1] **spike**: something that is long and thin with a sharp point

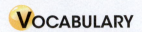

VOCABULARY

MEANING

Write the correct words in the blanks.

bite	dangerous	enemies	pattern	raw
chefs	dish	flavor	poison	

1. When you eat a blowfish, you can die. Its body is full of _____.

2. Most blowfish have bright colors. That is how their _____ know blowfish can kill.

3. The blowfish has no special taste. It has no special _____.

4. The Japanese _____ who prepare *fugu* have to train for three years.

5. *Fugu* is very expensive because this _____ is very difficult to prepare.

6. The blowfish does not need to be cooked. People eat it _____.

7. Eating blowfish can be _____. Twenty people die each year from eating blowfish.

8. You don't have to eat a lot of blowfish to die. Just one _____ of blowfish can kill you.

9. Some plates have a design such as a bird or flower. This is a _____.

WORDS THAT GO TOGETHER

Write the correct words in the blanks.

blows itself up	in danger	show off

1. The blowfish has this name because it _____ with air or water into a ball.

2. The blowfish is not always like a ball. It only does this when it feels _____.

3. People eat blowfish because it is dangerous and expensive. They want to _____.

USE

Work with a partner to answer the questions. Use complete sentences.

1. What food do you eat *raw*?
2. Who do you call when you are *in danger*?
3. Where does a *chef* work?
4. What animals can be *dangerous*?
5. What's your favorite *flavor* of ice cream?
6. What's your favorite *dish*?

COMPREHENSION

UNDERSTANDING THE READING

Circle the letter of the correct answer.

1. The blowfish is _____.

   a. a loved but dangerous fish to eat
   b. never served in restaurants
   c. a good fish for everyone to cook and eat

2. People eat blowfish because _____.

   a. it has a lot of taste
   b. they like the danger
   c. it is easy to buy for ordinary people

3. To prepare blowfish, a chef must _____.

   a. give a test to the person who wants to eat it
   b. follow strict rules
   c. work in a restaurant that has a certificate

REMEMBERING DETAILS

Reread the passage and answer the questions.

1. Where do most blowfish live?
2. Why do blowfish have bright colors?
3. What happens to many chefs who take the official test?
4. Where does the chef put the parts of the fish that have poison?
5. What does the chef use to cut the meat of the fish?
6. How does blowfish make people feel when they eat it?

SENTENCE COMPLETION

Match the words in column A and column B to make sentences.

A	B
____ 1. Only special chefs can prepare	a. following strict rules.
____ 2. Special chefs train	b. blowfish in a restaurant.
____ 3. The chef prepares the blowfish	c. on a beautiful plate.
____ 4. The Japanese pay a lot of money	d. for three years.
____ 5. The chef cuts	e. for a blowfish dinner.
____ 6. He serves the raw fish	f. the meat as thin as paper.

DICTATION

Work with a partner. Read three sentences from the exercise above. Your partner listens and writes the sentences. Then your partner reads three sentences and you write them.

DISCUSSION

Discuss the answers to these questions with your classmates.

1. What other types of seafood do the Japanese like to eat? Do people in your country eat seafood? What kinds of seafood are popular? What other foods are popular?

2. What are some unusual foods that people eat around the world? Do you eat any unusual foods? Would you like to try some? What would you like to try? What would you never want to eat?

3. The blowfish protects itself by blowing itself up into a ball and by being full of poison. What are some ways that other animals protect themselves?

CRITICAL THINKING

Work with a partner. Ask each other the following questions. Discuss your answers.

1. The chef prepares and serves blowfish in a special way; it's a special dish. What dishes in your country are prepared or served in a special way? How does the way we prepare and serve food make us feel about it? Is the way food is served important to you? Why or why not?

2. What do you think of people who eat blowfish? What are they like, do you think? Would you like to eat blowfish? Why?

WRITING

Complete the sentences about a special dish in your country.

EXAMPLE One of the special dishes in my country is <u>*roast lamb with rice stuffing*</u> .

1. One of the special dishes in my country is _____.

2. We do not eat this dish every week; we eat it _____.

3. We prepare this dish _____.

4. We serve this dish _____.

5. I like/don't like this dish because _____.

SPELLING AND PUNCTUATION

PLURALS: NOUNS ENDING IN -Y

Some singular nouns end in **-y**. To make these nouns **plural**, look at the **letter before the -y**.

*   If the letter is a **vowel**, add **-s**.
    day—days   *way—ways*

*   If the letter is a **consonant**, change the **-y** to **-i**, and add **-es**.
    enemy—enemies   *city—cities*

Underline the misspelled words. Write the correct words on the lines.

1. We eat a special dish at partys.   _____

2. You cannot give this food to babyes.   _____

3. My mother makes this for birthdayies.   _____

4. There are some strange storys about this dish.   _____

5. Familyes go to a restaurant for this dish.   _____

6. Some companyes are selling the fish for this dish. _____

 Go to page 137 for the Internet Activity.

DID YOU KNOW?	• **Blowfish are not very fast swimmers.** • **New Yorkers eat about one ton of blowfish every year.** • **Fugu is sold alive, so special arrangements must be made for transportation.** • **Lanterns made of fugu skin hang outside fugu restaurants in Japan.**

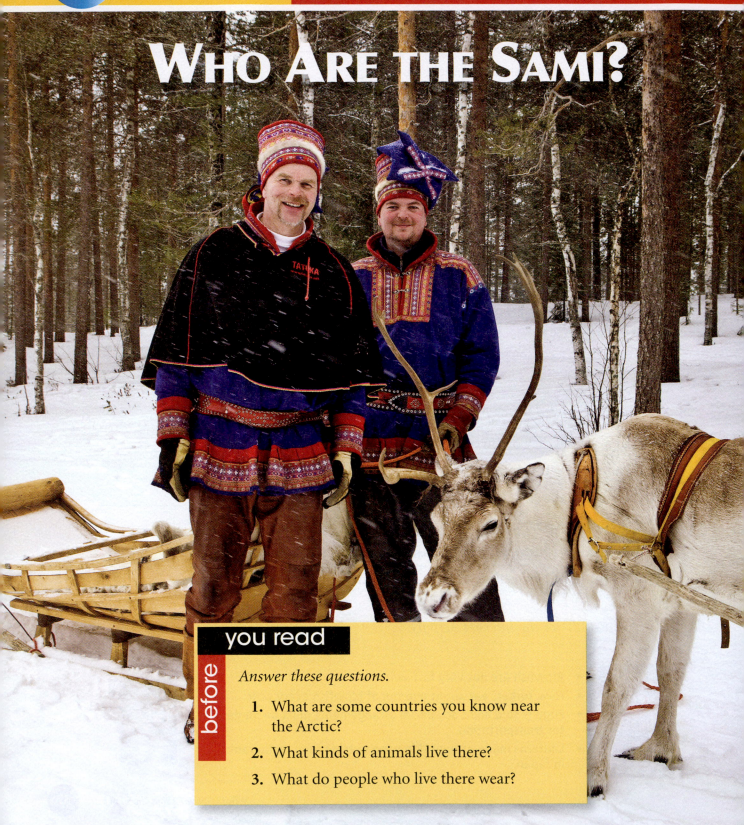

WHO ARE THE SAMI?

before you read

Answer these questions.

1. What are some countries you know near the Arctic?

2. What kinds of animals live there?

3. What do people who live there wear?

WHO ARE THE SAMI?

1   The Sami (also known as *Lapps*) are the native or original people of Sapmi (also known as *Lapland*). Sapmi is a region of northern Europe that covers parts of Norway, Sweden, Finland, and Russia. The Sami have lived there for thousands of years. They have their own languages, **culture**, and flag. There are about 100,000 Sami today.

2   The most important part of Sami culture is the reindeer. A long time ago, the Sami hunted[1] wild reindeer. Then they started herding[2] the reindeer. The Sami moved from place to place with the animals. It was their way of life. Some Samis still herd reindeer, but now they do it with **snowmobiles** and **helicopters**. Today, in Sapmi, only Sami people **are allowed to** herd reindeer.

3   Who is a Sami today? A person is a Sami if he or she **regards himself or herself** a Sami and has one parent or grandparent who learned Sami as his or her **native language**. More than half of the Sami speak Sami. There are several Sami languages. These languages are related, but Sami people who live far apart frequently cannot understand each other. Sami languages are old and have many words to **describe** nature. For example, there are more than ten words to describe snow. However, there are no words to describe **modern equipment**. Today most Sami are **bilingual**. They speak a Sami language and the language of the country they live in.

4   The Sami have traditional **costumes**. Each costume tells where the person wearing it comes from. The Sami wear their costumes on special occasions or when they are herding reindeer. Sami clothing has bright colors and patterns. These represent nature. Sami clothing lets others know if a person is single or married. For example, if the buttons on the belt are square, the person is married. If the buttons are round, the person is single.

5   Samis have traditional songs called *joiks*. When a Sami is born, a *joik* is made for the baby. It is the child's **personal** song for life. There are *joiks* to animals and birds, and to special people or special occasions. They can be happy or sad.

6   The Sami have their own flag. It stands for nature. Its colors are red for the sun, blue for the moon, and yellow and green for the land. The Sami feel very close to nature and are a **peaceful** people. Some say they are the only people that has never gone to war.

---

[1] **hunted**: chased wild animals in order to kill them
[2] **herding**: making animals move together as a group

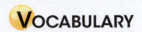

MEANING

Write the correct words in the blanks.

bilingual	culture	helicopters	personal
costumes	describe	peaceful	snowmobiles

1. Most Sami speak two languages well. They are _____.

2. The Sami languages have ten different words to _____ snow.

3. Each Sami child has his or her own _____ song.

4. The Sami wear their traditional _____ on special occasions.

5. The Sami do not like war. They are _____ people.

6. The reindeer is an important part of their _____.

7. The Sami do not drive cars on the snow. They drive _____.

8. They use snowmobiles and _____ to herd their reindeer.

WORDS THAT GO TOGETHER

Write the correct words in the blanks.

are allowed to	native language
modern equipment	regards himself or herself

1. The Sami use _____, but they do not have words for this equipment in their old languages.

2. A Sami is someone who _____ a Sami.

3. A Sami is also someone whose first language, or _____, is Sami.

4. The government does not give permission to other people to herd reindeer. Only the Sami _____ herd reindeer.

USE

Work with a partner to answer the questions. Use complete sentences.

1. What is your *native language*?
2. Which *modern equipment* do you use the most every day?
3. What is something that you *are* not *allowed to* do in class?
4. How do you *describe* yourself? Use two adjectives.
5. Do you wear a traditional *costume* on special occasions?
6. Who do you talk to about *personal* problems?

COMPREHENSION

UNDERSTANDING THE READING

Circle the letter of the correct answer.

1. The Sami have _____.
   a. a modern culture and an old language
   b. a traditional culture with some ties to the modern world
   c. an old culture with no knowledge of the modern world

2. The Sami people speak _____.
   a. a new language that changes all the time
   b. several languages that are related
   c. a single traditional language

3. The traditional clothing of the Sami _____.
   a. has one bright color and pattern
   b. is what they wear every day
   c. tells something about the person wearing it

REMEMBERING DETAILS

Reread the passage and answer the questions.

1. In what countries do the Sami live?
2. What do the Sami use today to help them herd reindeer?
3. What do the Sami languages have many words to describe?
4. What do the colors and patterns of the traditional Sami costumes represent?
5. After a *joik* is made for a baby, what does it become?
6. What are the colors on the Sami flag, and what do the colors mean?

SENTENCE COMPLETION

Match the words in column A and column B to make sentences.

	A		B
_____	**1.** The costume tells	**a.**	with many words to describe nature.
_____	**2.** The Sami are	**b.**	where the Sami comes from.
_____	**3.** The Sami languages are old	**c.**	a peaceful people.
_____	**4.** They wear their costumes	**d.**	culture and flag.
_____	**5.** The Sami have their own	**e.**	don't like war.
_____	**6.** The Sami are peaceful and	**f.**	on special occasions.

DICTATION

Work with a partner. Read three sentences from the exercise above. Your partner listens and writes the sentences. Then your partner reads three sentences and you write them.

DISCUSSION

Discuss the answers to these questions with your classmates.

1. What is an important animal in your culture? Why is it important?

2. What are some traditional costumes and customs in your country? What customs do you like the most? Why?

3. Is there snow in your country? Do you like snow and cold weather? What kinds of things can you do in places where there is a lot of snow? Which do you prefer, a warm or cold climate? Why?

CRITICAL THINKING

Work with a partner. Ask each other the following questions. Discuss your answers.

1. What is your native language? What languages do people speak in your country? Do you think it is important to speak more than one language? Why or why not?

2. The Sami are peaceful and feel close to nature. Would you like to see all cultures be like the Sami? Why or why not? What are some other cultures that have respect for nature? What do you admire most about the people of your country?

WRITING

Complete the sentences about the Sami.

EXAMPLE   The Sami live *in a region of northern Europe* _____.

1. The Sami have their own _____.

2. Their traditional costumes _____.

3. A long time ago, the Sami _____.

4. Today, most Sami speak _____.

5. The Sami love _____.

SPELLING AND PUNCTUATION

VERBS WITH *-ED* OR *-ING*

> Many verbs end in *-e*. We usually **drop the *-e*** before we **add *-ed* or *-ing***.
>
> *live + -ed = liv**ed***   *The Sami have liv**ed** in Sapmi for thousands of years.*
> *ride + -ing = rid**ing***   *He was rid**ing** his snowmobile when he fell.*

Circle the correctly spelled word for each sentence. You may use a dictionary.

1. They (movied / moved) from place to place.

2. Some women are still (making / makeing) costumes.

3. The Sami have (survivd / survived) for a long time.

4. The Sami have always (loved / loveed) nature.

5. We are (hoping / hopeing) to visit Sapmi this summer.

6. They are (comeing / coming) together for a special celebration.

7. Norway, Sweden, and Finland (recognized / recognizied) February 6 as Sami National Day.

Go to page 137 for the Internet Activity.

DID YOU KNOW?	• The Sami have lived in Norway longer than the Norwegians. They are Norway's original population. • Sami wear traditional clothing made of felt fabric. Felt keeps out the cold.	

WHY ARE RAIN FORESTS IMPORTANT?

before you read

Answer these questions.

1. Where can we find rain forests?

2. What kinds of animals live in rain forests?

3. Do you know a plant that comes from the rain forest?

WHY ARE
RAIN FORESTS IMPORTANT?

1   They are important for many reasons. Here are three of them: a great variety of plants and animals live in the rain forests; many of these plants and animals give us food and medicine; the rain forests help to **balance** the world's **climate**.

2   The rain forests cover less than 6 percent of the Earth's surface, which **includes** the oceans. They are in the tropics, that is, in hot, wet parts of the world. The largest rain forests are in South America around the Amazon River. There are other rain forests in central Africa, southeastern Asia, and on some Pacific islands. These rain forests support more than 50 percent of all life on the **planet**. The rain forests could have 50 million species or kinds of plants and animals. We do not know most of them yet.

3   Rain forests have many more species of plants than ordinary forests (for instance, 210 species of trees in 1 acre, instead of 20). We use many of these plants for food and medicine. Today, 80 percent of the fruits, vegetables, and spices we eat come from the rain forest. Also, 25 percent of the **drugs** we use come from rain forest plants. There are a lot more that we could use for food or to **cure** diseases like cancer or AIDS, but so far scientists have only studied 1 percent of these plants.

4   Rain forests have many more species of animals, too. For example, in the United States there are 81 species of frogs. But in Madagascar, which has a rain forest, there are 300 species of frogs. Some of these animals only live in rain forests. If we cut down the rain forests, they will die, and the species will disappear forever. Some of the animals in the rain forests give us important medicines **as well**.

5   The rain forests help to balance our climate. The trees in the rain forests remove carbon dioxide from the **atmosphere**. They produce oxygen for us. They put water in the atmosphere and help us to get rain. They balance our temperature so it is not too hot or too cold. They will help protect us from **global warming**, too.

6   Rain forests are disappearing very quickly. Humans are destroying 78 million acres of rain forest a year. That's about **the size of** Poland. What can we do? Well, we need to stop **harming** something so important for our future on Earth. We need to start protecting the rain forests and our **environment**.

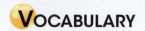 **V**OCABULARY

MEANING

Write the correct words in the blanks.

atmosphere	climate	drugs	harming	planet
balance	cure	environment	includes	

1. The Amazon rain forest has a hot, wet, and rainy _____.

2. The rain forest helps to _____ the world's climate, or keep the climate from sudden changes from hot to cold or cold to hot.

3. The rain forests cover 6 percent of _____ Earth.

4. All the rain forests are part of the 6 percent. It _____ all the rain forests.

5. When we cut down the rain forest, we are destroying or _____ our future.

6. We need to protect the air, the water, and the land, or our _____.

7. The rain forest takes out the carbon dioxide from the air around the Earth, or the _____.

8. There are plants in the rain forest that can make illnesses better or _____ diseases.

9. About 25 percent of the medicine, or _____, we use come from the rain forest.

WORDS THAT GO TOGETHER

Write the correct words in the blanks.

as well	global warming	the size of

1. The rain forest helps us against the rise in the Earth's temperature, or _____.

2. The rain forest gives us food. It gives us medicine _____.

3. Every year, we are destroying rain forests _____ Poland.

USE

Work with a partner to answer the questions. Use complete sentences.

1. What diseases can't we *cure*?
2. What kind of *climate* does your country have?
3. Is there something we can do to protect the Earth from *global warming*?
4. English pronunciation is difficult. What is difficult in English *as well*?
5. What is *the size of* your country?
6. What does a weekend *include*?

COMPREHENSION

UNDERSTANDING THE READING

Circle the letter of the correct answer.

1. Rain forests _____.

    a. are rich in plant and animal life
    b. cover much of the world's surface
    c. grow in northern areas of the world

2. Rain forests have _____.

    a. many important uses
    b. thousands of acres of one kind of tree
    c. 50 million kinds of plants that scientists know about

3. The trees in a rain forest _____.

    a. stop too much rain from falling on the Earth
    b. help us to breathe and stay cool
    c. give us problems of global warming

REMEMBERING DETAILS

*Circle **T** if the sentence is true. Circle **F** if the sentence is false.*

1. Rain forests cover nearly 20 percent of the Earth.   T   F

2. The largest rain forests are in South America.   T   F

3. An ordinary forest has more kinds of trees than a rain forest.   T   F

4. Scientists have found plants that can cure cancer and AIDS.   T   F

5. Madagascar has 300 species of frogs.   T   F

6. Rain forests take carbon dioxide out of the atmosphere.   T   F

SENTENCE COMPLETION

Match the words in column A and column B to make sentences.

A	B
_____ 1. The largest rain forest is in	a. give us food and medicine.
_____ 2. The rain forest is good	b. disappearing quickly.
_____ 3. Plants and animals in the rain forest	c. come from rain forest plants.
_____ 4. Twenty-five percent of our drugs	d. South America.
_____ 5. There are many kinds of trees	e. for our climate.
_____ 6. Rain forests are	f. in 1 acre of rain forest.

DICTATION

Work with a partner. Read three sentences from the exercise above. Your partner listens and writes the sentences. Then your partner reads three sentences and you write them.

DISCUSSION

Discuss the answers to these questions with your classmates.

1. Do you have rain forests or other kinds of forests in your country? Are they important to your country? Why or why not? How much does it rain in your country? When is the rainy season?

2. What are some animals that are native to your country? Where do they live? What animals are protected by laws? Do you think there should be laws to protect some animals? Why or why not?

3. What do you think will happen if people continue to destroy the rain forests? What can we do to protect them?

CRITICAL THINKING

Work with a partner. Ask each other the following questions. Discuss your answers.

1. What natural resources (for example, forests, minerals, and oil) does your country have? Do people harm the environment when they try to get those resources? Is it more important to protect the environment or get the natural resources? Why?

2. In what other ways are people harming the environment? What changes are happening around the world because of what humans have done? Do you think we can save our environment before it is too late? Why or why not?

WRITING

Complete the sentences about rain forests.

EXAMPLE   Rain forests cover *less than 6 percent of the Earth's surface*_____.

1. Rain forests give us_____.

2. Rain forests are in_____.

3. Some animals in the rain forest_____.

4. Rain forests help to_____.

5. Today, rain forests_____.

SPELLING AND PUNCTUATION

CAPITAL LETTERS: ABBREVIATIONS

An *abbreviation* is a short way to write a word, a phrase, or a name. Some abbreviations contain **all capital letters**. Each capital letter is the first letter of a word. This type of abbreviation can be **pronounced in two ways**.

- Some are pronounced as **one word**:
  AIDS   *Acquired Immune Deficiency Syndrome*
  NATO   *North Atlantic Treaty Organization*

- Others are pronounced as **separate letters**:
  NYU   *New York University*
  BBC   *British Broadcasting Corporation*

Abbreviations like these take a **singular verb**.
   AIDS **is** *a terrible disease.*

A. *Write the abbreviation next to each name. You may use a dictionary and/or the Internet.*

1. English as a Second Language   _____

2. Automated Teller Machine   _____

3. National Aeronautics and Space Administration   _____

4. Federal Bureau of Investigation   _____

5. Columbia Broadcasting System   _____

6. Internal Revenue Service   _____

7. United Nations Educational, Scientific, and
   Cultural Organization   _____

B. *Circle the correct form of the verb in parentheses.*

1. The FBI (investigate/investigates) crime in the United States.

2. The UN (was/were) started in 1945.

3. NASA (send/sends) astronauts to the international space station.

4. The USA (has/have) fifty states.

5. The CIA (collect/collects) information about other countries.

Go to page 137 for the Internet Activity.

| **DID YOU KNOW?** | • The trees of the Amazon rain forest have their roots in 9 countries (Peru, Brazil, Colombia, Venezuela, Ecuador, Bolivia, Guyana, Suriname, French Guiana).
• It rains every day in a rain forest.
• The trees are so dense in a rain forest that when it rains it takes as long as 10 minutes for the rain to reach the ground. |  |

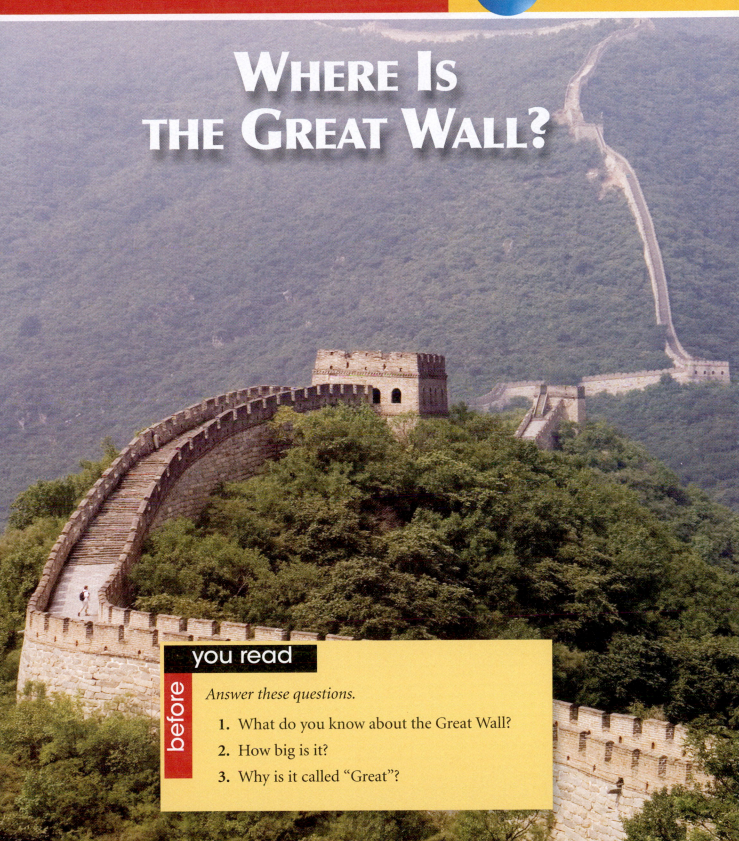

WHERE IS THE GREAT WALL?

you read

Answer these questions.

1. What do you know about the Great Wall?
2. How big is it?
3. Why is it called "Great"?

WHERE IS THE GREAT WALL?

1   The Great Wall is in China, north of Beijing. The Chinese built the Great Wall thousands of years ago. They wanted to protect their country from enemies coming from the north. First, they built small walls around their towns. Then the emperor, Shi Huangdi (221 B.C.–206 B.C.), joined the walls and built new parts. He wanted to make one long wall—the Great Wall.

2   Shi Huangdi was the first Qin emperor. The name *Qin* sounds like *Chin*. The word *China* **comes from** the name *Qin*. Shi Huangdi made many changes in China. He wanted China to be strong and modern. But many Chinese did not like Shi Huangdi. He didn't **care about** the people. Many people died because of his changes. Thousands of men worked on the Great Wall. It was very hard work. Many men got sick and died. Over 1 million people died building that **structure**. Their bodies are **buried** in the wall. Some people say the Great Wall is "the Wall of Death."

3   Other Chinese emperors **added** to the wall and made it better. The Ming emperors added thousands of tall, strong buildings in the years 1368–1644. Men stayed in the buildings to protect and repair the wall. They were called guards. Sometimes more than a million guards worked on the wall. They were born on the wall and **grew up** there. They married there and died there. Many guards lived on the Great Wall all their lives. When enemies **attacked** a part of the wall, the guards made a fire to show they needed help. Guards from other parts of the wall ran **along** the top of the wall to help them.

4   We don't know **exactly** how long the Great Wall is. There are many different parts of the wall, and some parts **fell down**. The Great Wall is about 4,000 miles (6,400 kilometers) long and about 25 feet (7.6 meters) high. It is about 15 feet (4.6 meters) wide at the top. Buses and cars can drive along parts of the wall. Today, the Great Wall is the largest **monument** in the world. Some people say you can see the Great Wall from **space**. But in 1969, an astronaut who traveled in space said he did not see any buildings on Earth—not even the Great Wall.

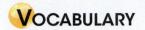

MEANING

Write the correct words in the blanks.

added	attacked	exactly	space
along	buried	monument	structure

1. How long is the Great Wall? We are not quite sure. We don't know

    _____ how long it is.

2. Some emperors put new parts onto the wall. They _____ to it.

3. The wall protected the people when enemies _____ them.

4. An astronaut in _____ did not see the Great Wall. He was very far

    up in the sky away from the Earth.

5. The Chinese built something very big. They built a big _____.

6. On one part of the wall, you can drive a car or bus from one end to the other. You

    can drive _____ the top of the wall.

7. The stones and rocks in the wall covered some men's bodies. The bodies were

    _____.

8. A building that is important for historical reasons is a _____.

WORDS THAT GO TOGETHER

Write the correct words in the blanks.

care about	comes from	fell down	grew up

1. Some parts of the wall _____. The parts dropped to the ground.

2. Some words are developed from other words. The word *China*

    _____ the name *Qin*.

3. Many guards lived on the wall as children. They stayed there and became adults.

    They _____ on the wall.

4. He was not interested in his people. He did not _____ them.

USE

Work with a partner to answer the questions. Use complete sentences.

1. Where did you *grow up*?
2. When *exactly* did you move to your home?
3. Does your country have a famous *monument*?
4. What is the largest *structure* in your city?
5. What can you see in *space*?
6. Who do you *care about* very much?

COMPREHENSION

UNDERSTANDING THE READING

Circle the letter of the correct answer.

1. China's first Qin emperor _____.

   a. joined the small walls
   b. put a million guards at the wall
   c. made the first small wall

2. Guards protected the wall from _____.

   a. enemies
   b. the emperor
   c. other guards

3. An astronaut in space _____.

   a. saw part of the wall
   b. saw the whole wall
   c. did not see the wall

REMEMBERING DETAILS

Circle T if the sentence is true. Circle F if the sentence is false.

1. The Ming emperors made the first wall.	T	F
2. The word *China* comes from the name of the first Qin emperor.	T	F
3. Over 1 million people died building the wall.	T	F
4. Guards protected and repaired the wall.	T	F
5. A bus can drive along certain parts of the top of the wall.	T	F
6. The wall is about 400 miles long.	T	F

SENTENCE COMPLETION

Match the words in column A and column B to make sentences.

A	**B**
____ 1. The Great Wall is	**a.** many changes in China.
____ 2. Many guards lived	**b.** the largest monument in the world.
____ 3. The first emperor made	**c.** on the wall all their lives.
____ 4. The Chinese wanted	**d.** thousands of tall, strong buildings.
____ 5. Sometimes enemies	**e.** to protect their country.
____ 6. The Ming emperors added	**f.** attacked a part of the wall.

DICTATION

Work with a partner. Read three sentences from the exercise above. Your partner listens and writes the sentences. Then your partner reads three sentences and you write them.

DISCUSSION

Discuss the answers to these questions with your classmates.

1. What is the biggest structure or building in your country?
2. Many important buildings are big. Some important buildings are small. What is a small, important building?
3. Do you like new buildings or old buildings? Why?

CRITICAL THINKING

Work with a partner. Ask each other the following questions. Discuss your answers.

1. Do you think the Great Wall was a good thing for China? Why or why not? What do walls between countries and neighbors do? How are they good? How are they bad?
2. Do you think it is important to spend money on keeping and restoring monuments like the Great Wall? Why or why not?

Complete the sentences about the Great Wall.

EXAMPLE   The Great Wall is *in China, north of Beijing* _____ .

1. The Chinese built _____ .

2. Shi Huangdi _____ .

3. Emperors added _____ .

4. Many guards _____ .

5. Today, the Great Wall is _____ .

Spelling and Punctuation

CAPITAL LETTERS: IMPORTANT STRUCTURES AND MONUMENTS

> We use a **capital letter** for the **main words** in the name of an **important structure** or **monument**. We do **NOT** use a capital letter for the words *the* or *of* in the name.
>
> *Some people say the **Great Wall** is the **Wall** of **Death**.*

Underline and correct the words that need capital letters. Remember the capital letter rules from other units.

1. In beijing, china, the temple of heaven is one of the most beautiful sights.

2. At one time, the eiffel tower in paris, france was the tallest structure in the world.

3. Later, the empire state building in new york became the tallest structure.

4. In 1976, the CN tower in toronto, canada became the tallest tower in the world.

5. The gateway arch in st. louis, missouri is the highest monument in the world.

6. The tallest statue in the world is amida buddha in ushiku city, japan.

Go to page 138 for the Internet Activity.

DID YOU KNOW?
- The Chinese used rice flour to hold the bricks together when they were building the Great Wall.
- Shi Huangdi never spent more than two days in the same place in case people tried to kill him.

WHAT IS TORNADO ALLEY?

before **you read**

Answer these questions.

1. What is a tornado?
2. Where do tornadoes occur?
3. What kind of damage can a tornado do?

What Is Tornado Alley?

1   Tornado Alley is a **nickname** for an **area** in the center of the United States. This area has the most tornadoes. It also has the strongest and most dangerous tornadoes. Tornado Alley includes parts of Texas, Oklahoma, Kansas, and Nebraska. The area is not always exactly the same. It can change **depending on** where the most tornadoes take place. Texas gets about 110 each year. One city— Oklahoma City, Oklahoma—had 33 tornadoes in the last ninety years! Not every city in Tornado Alley has had a tornado, but some cities have had tornadoes many times.

2   If you live in Tornado Alley, the time to watch the sky is from late March to June. If the sky turns black, there are clouds near the ground, and there is a big **thunderstorm** coming, run for the storm cellar! A storm cellar is a safe place or **shelter**. Some storm cellars are in the **basement** of the home. Others are underground structures near the home. If you do not have a storm cellar, go to the middle of the house into a **closet** or a bathroom.

3   Do you remember the movie *The Wizard of Oz*? A tornado comes to Kansas and lifts Dorothy's house high into the air. Can this really happen? One woman in Oklahoma saw a tornado. It was **coming her way**. She immediately took her two children and the dog to the bathroom and jumped into the bathtub. Then they covered their heads with a **mattress**. At first, they heard a **sound** like a train. Then there were **explosions**. Finally, they heard the sound of strong rain on their mattress. When they pushed the mattress away and looked up, there was no house. The house was gone. The only things left were the mattress, the bathtub, the mother, the two children, and the dog.

4   The biggest tornado outbreak happened in 1974. A tornado outbreak is when there are six or more tornadoes at the same time. That year, there were 148 tornadoes in thirteen states in sixteen hours. There were 330 people killed and almost 5,500 people injured. Something like this is rare, but scientists say it can come back again. However, we know that the next time there won't be so many people killed or injured. That's because, today, we have a much better **warning system**.

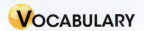

VOCABULARY

MEANING

Write the correct words in the blanks.

area	closet	mattress	shelter	thunderstorm
basement	explosions	nickname	sound	

1. To sleep well, you need a bed with a good _____.

2. When you hear a loud noise and see a flash of lightning in the sky, it is a(n) _____.

3. When you don't have a storm cellar, you can go into a _____— a small room where you usually keep your clothes.

4. A _____ is the part of a building that is below the level of the ground.

5. They heard something. It was a _____ like a train.

6. When the tornado was over them, there were _____, or very loud noises like bombs bursting into small pieces.

7. Tornado Alley is a(n) _____ at the center of the United States.

8. Tornado Alley is a name or _____ people use for that area.

9. A safe place to go to in bad weather or a tornado is a _____.

WORDS THAT GO TOGETHER

Write the correct words in the blanks.

coming her way	depending on	warning system

1. She saw the black sky and the big clouds near the ground. A tornado was _____.

2. Today, we know when a tornado is coming. We have a _____.

3. The area of Tornado Alley can change _____ where there are the most tornadoes.

USE

Work with a partner to answer the questions. Use complete sentences.

1. Do you have a *nickname*? What is it?
2. What *sounds* do you hear right now?
3. What do you have in your *closet*?
4. Where do you put a *mattress*?
5. When do you usually hear an *explosion*?
6. When do you get *thunderstorms*?

COMPREHENSION

UNDERSTANDING THE READING

Circle the letter of the correct answer.

1. Tornado Alley is an area _____.

   a. that is on the map and includes six states

   b. that has the most tornadoes

   c. where every city has had a tornado

2. If a tornado is coming, you must _____.

   a. run quickly out of the area

   b. stay outside and away from the house

   c. find a safe place or shelter

3. A tornado outbreak is _____.

   a. something that happens often in Tornado Alley

   b. when one powerful tornado hits many different places at once

   c. when many tornadoes hit a large area in a short time

REMEMBERING DETAILS

Circle **T** *if the sentence is true. Circle* **F** *if the sentence is false.*

1. Texas gets about 33 tornadoes every year.   T   F

2. Oklahoma City had 33 tornadoes in 1999.   T   F

3. Tornadoes in Tornado Alley happen between June and August.   T   F

4. Some storm cellars are below the house.   T   F

5. A woman and her two children found shelter in a bathtub.   T   F

6. In 1974, there were 300 tornadoes in twenty-four hours.   T   F

SENTENCE COMPLETION

Match the words in column A and column B to make sentences.

	A		**B**
_____	1. The family covered their heads	a.	jumped into the bathtub.
_____	2. The time to watch the sky is	b.	with a mattress.
_____	3. A woman took her two children and	c.	on their mattress.
_____	4. They heard	d.	there was no house.
_____	5. They heard the sound of strong rain	e.	from late March to June.
_____	6. When they looked up,	f.	a loud sound like a train.

DICTATION

Work with a partner. Read three sentences from the exercise above. Your partner listens and writes the sentences. Then your partner reads three sentences and you write them.

Ｄ ISCUSSION

Discuss the answers to these questions with your classmates.

1. What kind of bad storms do you have in your country? How do you know when a storm is coming? If a storm comes, what do you do?

2. What area of your country is the most dangerous to live in? What area of your country is not dangerous? Why?

3. What was the worst natural disaster (tornado, hurricane, flood, earthquake, etc.) to happen in your country? When did it happen? Did people know it was coming?

CRITICAL THINKING

Work with a partner. Ask each other the following questions. Discuss your answers.

1. Some people go to where there are tornadoes or hurricanes happening and photograph them. These people are called *storm chasers*. Do you think these people are foolish or brave? Why? Why do you think they do this dangerous work? Would you like to do something dangerous like that? Why or why not?

2. Many people live in Tornado Alley. Other people live near rivers that flood or in areas that have many fires. What are some other dangerous areas to live in? Why do you think people live in these places? Why do people build their homes again in the same place?

WRITING

Complete the sentences about Tornado Alley.

EXAMPLE   Tornado Alley is a nickname _for an area in the center of the U.S._.

1. Tornado Alley has _____.

2. The time to watch for tornadoes is _____.

3. A storm cellar is _____.

4. A tornado outbreak is _____.

5. Today, it is safer than before because _____.

SPELLING AND PUNCTUATION

COMMAS: ITEMS IN A SERIES

We use a **comma** between words or phrases in a **series of three or more**.
*Tornado Alley includes parts of **Texas, Oklahoma, Kansas, and Nebraska**.*
*The time to watch out for tornadoes is **early spring, late spring, and early summer**.*

We do **NOT** use a comma between **two words or phrases** in a series.
***Texas and Oklahoma** get a lot of tornadoes.*
***Pieces of wood and scraps of metal** were flying through the air.*

Write **C** *for sentences that are correct. Insert commas where necessary in incorrect sentences.*

_____ 1. The only things left were the mattress, the bathtub, the mother the two children and the dog.

_____ 2. Be careful when the clouds are dark and black.

_____ 3. Tornadoes can kill and injure people.

_____ 4. In Tornado Alley, the dangerous months are March April May and June.

_____ 5. A tornado can suck up animals, cars, people and houses.

_____ 6. Tornadoes hurricanes, earthquakes, floods and tsunamis are all dangerous.

_____ 7. A tornado's path is narrow and dangerous.

_____ 8. Lie face down and cover your head.

_____ 9. I heard the warning on the radio and the television.

_____ 10. People can take shelter in a storm cellar a bathroom or a closet.

_____ 11. There is a strong noise and a smell of rotting food as the tornado gets closer.

_____ 12. You know it's coming when the sky gets dark clouds that are near the ground and you hear thunder.

 Go to page 138 for the Internet Activity.

Go to page 138 for the Internet Activity.

| **DID YOU KNOW?** | • **Every tornado has its own color, sound, and shape.**
• **A tornado can occur at any time, but most often between 3 P.M. and 9 P.M.**
• **In 2008, in the first seven months of the year 1,389 tornadoes touched down in the U.S.** | |

SELF-TEST 1: UNITS 1–10

A. COMPREHENSION

Circle the letter of the correct answer.

1. J. K. Rowling _____.
   a. was wealthy and successful before she became a famous author
   b. had many hardships in her life before she wrote the *Harry Potter* books
   c. wrote several children's books before she wrote the *Harry Potter* books
   d. acted in movies before she became an author

2. The purpose of New Year traditions is to _____.
   a. give thanks
   b. bring families together
   c. bring wealth
   d. ask for forgiveness

3. For those living in Buckingham Palace, _____.
   a. there are many rules and traditions to follow
   b. there are parties almost every day
   c. they must live among tourists all year long
   d. life is dull since there are few things to do

4. The Indian government spends a lot of money caring for cows because _____.
   a. there are many people who want to kill them
   b. they are very special to the Indian people
   c. they use them to do work for the government
   d. they give them to farmers

5. Wedding gifts _____.
   a. always bring happiness and good fortune to the families of the bride and groom
   b. are meant to help couples, but can cause problems as well
   c. are against the law in many Middle Eastern countries
   d. are usually for the families of the couple

6. People eat blowfish because they _____.

   a. like its delicious taste

   b. do not believe it has poison in it

   c. think it's the most beautiful fish in the ocean

   d. want to show their courage and wealth

7. The Sami _____.

   a. usually live in cities and own businesses

   b. came to northern Europe only recently

   c. no longer speak their native language or follow their traditions

   d. are peaceful people who love nature

8. Rain forests _____.

   a. are common and cover much of the Earth

   b. have fewer plants and animals than other types of forests

   c. provide us with many foods and medicines

   d. are found in cold, northern areas of the globe

9. The Chinese emperors built the Great Wall to _____.

   a. protect themselves from enemies

   b. make a beautiful monument for everyone to see

   c. show how powerful they were

   d. keep the citizens from leaving the country

10. Tornado Alley is _____.

   a. the name of a movie that was about tornadoes

   b. a city in Oklahoma that has many tornadoes

   c. a place where people go to find shelter from tornadoes

   d. an area of the United States that has many dangerous tornadoes

B. VOCABULARY

Complete the definitions. Circle the letter of the correct answer.

1. She wrote a book. She is the _____.
   - **a.** adult
   - **b.** author
   - **c.** guest
   - **d.** foreigner

2. When people do things every year for many years, these things are _____
   - **a.** traditions
   - **b.** celebrations
   - **c.** parties
   - **d.** gifts

3. The palace has many rooms. It has _____ of rooms.
   - **a.** on top of
   - **b.** the same as
   - **c.** a lot of
   - **d.** a little of

4. You want something to look nice. You _____ it.
   - **a.** cost
   - **b.** eat
   - **c.** use
   - **d.** decorate

5. You have enough money to buy something. You can _____ it.
   - **a.** prepare
   - **b.** hit
   - **c.** afford
   - **d.** sell

6. When you do not cook food, you eat it _____.
   - **a.** dangerous
   - **b.** poisonous
   - **c.** raw
   - **d.** bright

7. When an authority or government gives you permission to do something, you are _____ to do it.
   - **a.** correct to
   - **b.** allowed to
   - **c.** respect to
   - **d.** regard to

8. To keep something equal on both sides is to _____ it.
   - **a.** cost
   - **b.** include
   - **c.** balance
   - **d.** cure

9. The place where you lived when you were young is the place where you _____.
   - **a.** grew up
   - **b.** came from
   - **c.** cared about
   - **d.** fell down

10. Most people sleep on a _____ on a bed for comfort.
    - **a.** mattress
    - **b.** shelter
    - **c.** closet
    - **d.** basement

C. SPELLING AND PUNCTUATION

Circle the letter of the sentence with the correct spelling and punctuation.

1. **a.** J. K. Rowling wrote *harry Potter*.

   b. J. K. Rowling wrote *Harry Potter*.

   c. J. k. Rowling wrote *Harry Potter*.

   d. J. K. Rowling wrote *harry potter*.

2. **a.** People celebrate New year's day around the world.

   b. People celebrate New year's Day around the world.

   c. People celebrate New Year's Day around the world.

   d. People celebrate New Year's day around the world.

3. **a.** Queen elizabeth lives in Buckingham Palace.

   b. Qween Elizabeth lives in Buckingham Palace.

   c. Queen Elizabeth lives in Buckingham Palace.

   d. Quween Elizabeth lives in Buckingham Palace.

4. **a.** The farms arn't busy at certain times.

   b. The farms are'nt busy at certain times.

   c. The farms aren't busy at certain times.

   d. The farms are'not busy at certain times.

5. **a.** They like Singer Sewing Machines in India.

   b. They like Singer sewing machines in India.

   c. They like singer sewing machines in India.

   d. They like Singer Sewing machines in India.

6. **a.** There are libraries in many cities.

   b. There are libraryes in many cities.

   c. They are libraries in many cityes.

   d. There are libraryies in many cityies.

7. **a.** The sami moved from place to place riding their snowmobiles.

   b. The Sami moved from place to place riding their snowmobiles.

   c. The Sami moved from place to place rideing their snowmobiles.

   d. The Sami movd from place to place ridding their snowmobiles.

8. **a.** She's an CBS reporter.

   b. She's a CBS reporter.

   c. She's a Cbs reporter.

   d. She's a C.B.S reporter.

9. **a.** The Great Wall Of China is the largest monument in the world.

   b. the Great Wall of China is the largest monument in the world.

   c. The Great Wall of China is the largest monument in the world.

   d. The great wall of china is the largest monument in the world.

10. **a.** March April May and June are dangerous months for tornadoes.

    b. March, April, May and June are dangerous months for tornadoes.

    c. March, April, May, and June are dangerous months for tornadoes.

    d. march, april, may, and june are dangerous months for tornadoes.

WHO WAS ANDREW CARNEGIE?

before you read

Answer these questions.

1. Andrew Carnegie was the richest man in the world in 1900. Who is the richest man in the world today?

2. How do people become rich?

3. What do rich people do with their money?

WHO WAS ANDREW CARNEGIE?

1   Andrew Carnegie was an extremely rich man who **gave away** all his money to help other people. Andrew Carnegie was born in 1835 in Scotland. He was from a poor family. When he was twelve, his family moved to the United States. They wanted a better life.

2   The Carnegie family lived in Pittsburgh, Pennsylvania. Andrew started to work **right away**. He got a job in a **factory**. He was a good worker, but he didn't like the job. Later, he changed his job. He worked at the Pennsylvania Railroad Company. Everybody there liked Andrew. He did many different jobs. His salary got higher every year.

3   In his free time, Andrew loved to read. But in those days, it was difficult to get books if you did not have money. The United States did not have free public libraries then. Fortunately, Andrew lived near Colonel James Anderson. Colonel Anderson was a rich man with many books, and he **let** working boys like Andrew use his library for free. Andrew read **as much as possible**. In fact, he read **throughout** his life. He always thought that reading was very important.

4   Andrew learned a lot at the railroad company. He **realized** that the railroad was very important for big countries. Then he had an idea: to start a business connected with the railroads. He **saved** all his money and opened that business. He was thirty years old.

5   First, his company made **bridges** for the railroads. Ten years later, they made steel. The Carnegie Steel Company became the largest company in the United States. They made steel for bridges, machines, and many other things. People called Carnegie the "Steel King." Soon he was the richest man in the world.

6   Carnegie liked to make money. But he believed the rich should help other people. In 1901, he sold his company for $480 million. Then he started to give away his money to build public libraries all over the United States and the English-speaking world. In all, he built 2,811 public libraries. Carnegie also gave millions of dollars to colleges, museums, scientific institutions, and people who worked for **peace**.

7   Andrew Carnegie died in 1919. He was eighty-four years old. During his lifetime, he gave away **nearly** all of his money for education and peace. Today, a foundation[1] **named after** him—the Carnegie Foundation—continues his work. Andrew Carnegie is still helping people all over the world to study and learn.

---

[1] *foundation:* an organization that gives or collects money to be used for special purposes

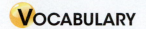

MEANING

Write the correct words in the blanks.

bridges	let	peace	saved
factory	nearly	realized	throughout

1. Andrew worked in a building where people made things. He worked in a

   _____.

2. Andrew read from the beginning to the end of his life. He read

   _____ his life.

3. Andrew _____ that the railroad was important. He knew and

   understood that this was true.

4. The trains on the railroad needed to go over rivers and roads. Carnegie made

   _____ for the railroad.

5. Carnegie did not want war or fighting. He wanted _____.

6. Carnegie kept his money to use later. He _____ his money.

7. Colonel Anderson wanted working boys to use his library. He allowed them to

   read the books. He _____ them use the library.

8. Carnegie gave almost all of his money for education and peace. He gave away

   _____ all his money.

WORDS THAT GO TOGETHER

Write the correct words in the blanks.

as much as possible	gave away	named after	right away

1. Andrew started to work immediately. He worked _____.

2. Carnegie wanted other people to have his money. He _____

   his money.

3. There is a Carnegie Library in Pittsburgh. It is _____

   Andrew Carnegie.

4. Carnegie was busy at the factory. Sometimes he had free time. He read in

   his free time. He read _____.

USE

Work with a partner to answer the questions. Use complete sentences.

1. Do you try to *save* money? What for?
2. What do you do *right away* after school or work?
3. What do you do *throughout* your school day?
4. What is the name of a famous *bridge*?
5. What is made in a *factory*?
6. Do you know a building *named after* someone famous? What is it?

COMPREHENSION

UNDERSTANDING THE READING

Circle the letter of the correct answer.

1. Andrew Carnegie opened his own _____.

   a. bridge   **b.** steel company   **c.** railroad

2. Andrew and other working boys went to _____.

   a. the factory   **b.** the public library   **c.** Colonel Anderson's library

3. Carnegie became the richest man in _____.

   a. Pittsburgh   **b.** the United States   **c.** the world

REMEMBERING DETAILS

Reread the passage and answer the questions.

1. Where was Andrew Carnegie born?
2. When did he start to work?
3. What did his first company make?
4. What did he make steel for?
5. When did he sell his company?
6. How many public libraries did he build?

UNDERSTANDING THE SEQUENCE

Which happened first? Write **1** on the line. Which happened second? Write **2** on the line.

1. _____ Carnegie worked at the Pennsylvania Railroad Company.

   _____ Carnegie worked in a factory.

2. _____ Carnegie made bridges for the railroads.

   _____ Carnegie made steel.

3. _____ Carnegie became the richest man in the world.

   _____ People called Carnegie the "Steel King."

4. _____ Carnegie built libraries and colleges.

   _____ Carnegie sold his company.

TELL THE STORY

Work with a partner. Tell the story of Andrew Carnegie to your partner. Use your own words. Your partner asks you questions about the story. Then your partner tells you the story and you ask questions.

DISCUSSION

Discuss the answers to these questions with your classmates.

1. Imagine you are the richest person in the world. What would you do with your money?
2. Does money always make people happy? Explain.
3. Carnegie's family was poor. Later, he made a lot of money. Do you know anyone like this? Tell his or her story.

CRITICAL THINKING

Work with a partner. Ask each other the following questions. Discuss your answers.

1. Why is reading important? How does reading help a person become successful? How does reading help someone become a better person? Do you like to read? Why or why not?
2. Imagine someone gave you a large amount of money only to help others. What institutions or people would you give money to, and why?

WRITING

Complete the sentences about Andrew Carnegie.

EXAMPLE   Carnegie was born *in Scotland* _____.

1. Carnegie worked _____.

2. Carnegie loved _____.

3. Carnegie started _____.

4. Carnegie became _____.

5. Carnegie gave _____.

SPELLING AND PUNCTUATION

NUMBERS AS WORDS

> The words ***hundred, thousand,*** and ***million*** are **plural** when there are **no numbers before** them.
>   *He gave away **millions** of dollars.*   *There are **hundreds** of people here.*
>
> When there is **a number before** them, they are **singular**.
>   *He gave away over **$350 million**.*   *There are **five hundred** people here.*
>
> We use a **hyphen (-) between two-word numbers** from *twenty-one* to *ninety-nine*.
>   ***thirty-one***   ***eighty-four***

*Write **C** for numbers with correct spelling and punctuation. Rewrite numbers with incorrect spelling or punctuation.*

____ **1.** ninety one   _____   ____ **4.** two thousands   _____

____ **2.** fiftytwo   _____   ____ **5.** twelve hundred   _____

____ **3.** thirty-five   _____   ____ **6.** three millions   _____

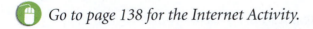 *Go to page 138 for the Internet Activity.*

Go to page 138 for the Internet Activity.

| **DID YOU KNOW?** | • Andrew Carnegie only attended four years of school in his entire life.
• Carnegie didn't want extravagant libraries, so he left guidelines for simple buildings.
• The Carnegie Foundation is the oldest and largest foundation in the world. |  |

WHAT IS LIFE LIKE IN ANTARCTICA?

before you read

Answer these questions.

1. What do you see in the picture?
2. Do you think people live there?
3. Would you like to visit Antarctica?

WHAT IS LIFE LIKE IN ANTARCTICA?

1   Antarctica is like no other place in the world. It is **unique**. It is very big—it is like the size of the United States and Australia together. It is also very cold. In fact, Antarctica is the coldest place in the world. The **temperature** sometimes falls to −125°F (−87°C). August and September are the coldest months because there is no sun.

2   Antarctica is at the southern tip of the world. It is the highest **continent**. It is 10,000 feet high. Antarctica also has very strong winds. The wind sometimes **blows** 200 miles an hour. It is also the driest place in the world. Antarctica is drier than the Sahara Desert!

3   Antarctica is also **empty**. There are **huge** glaciers and ice everywhere. A glacier is an area of ice that moves slowly. The ice and glaciers are beautiful. But most plants and land animals cannot live on the ice. It is too cold. There are no trees, no rivers, and no cities in Antarctica. There are no land animals. Only penguins and other sea birds live there.

4   Antarctica does not **belong to** any one country. In fact, every country owns Antarctica. More than twenty countries have stations in Antarctica. A station is a place where scientists do **experiments**. There are **separate** stations for different countries. The scientists are the only people who live in Antarctica. **In all**, over 4,000 people live at the stations in the summer. Over 1,000 people live there in the winter.

5   Life on an Antarctic station is hard. It is like life on a space station. The sun shines for six months, and then it is night for six months. People usually have problems with sleeping and eating. They eat more because they are not busy. In an emergency, it is hard to get help. In 1999, an American doctor named Jerri Nielsen realized she was sick. She had cancer. It was winter, and airplanes could not land in Antarctica. She was the only doctor there. Dr. Nielsen **had no choice**. She had to stay. An airplane **dropped** medicine to her, and she took care of herself. Several months later, Dr. Nielsen returned to the United States to get special medical help.

6   Today, more and more people visit Antarctica. Ships go to Antarctica during the summer months from November to February. People want to visit this unusual place, but they don't want to live there!

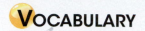

VOCABULARY

MEANING

Write the correct words in the blanks.

blows	dropped	experiments	separate	unique
continent	empty	huge	temperature	

1. The medicine fell from the plane. It _____ from the plane.

2. It is very cold in Antarctica. The _____ is sometimes −125°F (−87°C).

3. The wind _____ 200 miles an hour. The wind moves very fast.

4. There is nothing in Antarctica. It is _____.

5. The glaciers are very, very big. They are _____.

6. Scientists go to Antarctica to do special tests. They do _____.

7. Antarctica is different from the other continents. It is special. Antarctica is

   _____.

8. The stations are not joined together. They are _____ from each other.

9. The United States is a large country. It is on the _____ of North America.

WORDS THAT GO TOGETHER

Write the correct words in the blanks.

belong to	had no choice	in all

1. There were a total of 4,000 people there. There were 4,000 people

   _____.

2. Who owns Antarctica? Who does Antarctica _____?

3. Dr. Nielsen could not do anything else. She _____.

USE

Work with a partner to answer the questions. Use complete sentences.

1. What are the seven *continents*?
2. What is the *temperature* today?
3. How many people are in your family *in all*?
4. What kind of *experiments* do you find interesting?
5. When does the wind *blow* a lot?
6. What movie was a *huge* success this year?

COMPREHENSION

UNDERSTANDING THE READING

Circle the letter of the correct answer.

1. Antarctica belongs to _____.

   a. the United States   **b.** every country   **c.** twenty countries

2. Scientists live in Antarctica _____.

   a. in the summer   **b.** in the winter   **c.** in the summer and the winter

3. On an Antarctic station _____.

   a. people eat less   **b.** there is no space   **c.** life is difficult

REMEMBERING DETAILS

Circle T if the sentence is true. Circle F if the sentence is false.

1. Antarctica is drier than the Sahara Desert.   T   F

2. The wind blows 300 miles an hour.   T   F

3. Most plants and animals can live on the ice.   T   F

4. People have problems sleeping in Antarctica.   T   F

5. People visit Antarctica in July and August.   T   F

6. Penguins live in Antarctica.   T   F

SENTENCE COMPLETION

Match the words in column A and column B to make sentences.

A	B
_____ 1. Scientists live	**a.** the coldest place in the world.
_____ 2. Antarctica has	**b.** on stations in Antarctica.
_____ 3. Antarctica is	**c.** very strong winds.
_____ 4. The sun shines	**d.** experiments in Antarctica.
_____ 5. Scientists do	**e.** to one country.
_____ 6. Antarctica doesn't belong	**f.** for six months of the year.

DICTATION

Work with a partner. Read three sentences from the exercise above. Your partner listens and writes the sentences. Then your partner reads three sentences and you write them.

DISCUSSION

Discuss the answers to these questions with your classmates.

1. Do you want to visit Antarctica? Why or why not?
2. Antarctica is an unusual place to visit. What are other unusual places to visit?
3. What do you think scientists find in Antarctica?

CRITICAL THINKING

Work with a partner. Ask each other the following questions. Discuss your answers.

1. How do you think life on an Antarctic station is like life on a space station? What are some of the difficulties of living in these places? Would you be able to live in Antarctica or on a space station? Why or why not?
2. Imagine someone gives you a choice among three places to live. One place is a hot and dry desert. One is a hot and wet rain forest. One is a cold and windy ice sheet. Which place do you choose and why? What would be the good and bad points of living there?

WRITING

Complete the sentences about Antarctica.

EXAMPLE   Antarctica is _a continent_____.

1. Antarctica is _____.

2. Antarctica has _____.

3. There are _____.

4. Scientists _____.

5. People _____.

SPELLING AND PUNCTUATION

MONTHS IN THE YEAR

There are twelve **months** in the year. Usually, we write the **complete name**.
August and *September* are the coldest months.

Here are the names of the **twelve months** of the year.

January	*April*	*July*	*October*
February	*May*	*August*	*November*
March	*June*	*September*	*December*

Sometimes we shorten, or **abbreviate**, the **names of the months**. We often
abbreviate on forms or checks. We put a **period after** the abbreviation.
Date: _____ ***Dec.** 24, 2010_

Circle the correct abbreviation. You may use a dictionary.

1. **January**   Janu.   Jan.   Jany

2. **March**   Mar.   Mch.   Mach.

3. **May**   My   May.   *no abbreviation*

4. **July**   Jul.   Jly   *no abbreviation*

5. **September**   Sep.   Sept.   Spt.

 Go to page 139 for the Internet Activity.

DID YOU KNOW?	• Many Antarctic fish have antifreeze in their blood to survive the cold waters. • There are about 3 million icebergs in the Southern Ocean around Antarctica.	

WHERE DO PEOPLE LIVE UNDER THE GROUND?

before you read

Answer these questions.

1. Look at the picture. Where do these people live?

2. Why do you think they live under the ground?

3. Do you know other places in the world where people live under the ground?

WHERE DO PEOPLE LIVE UNDER THE GROUND?

1   One place where people live under the ground is a small town called Coober Pedy. Coober Pedy is in the outback of South Australia. Most of the people in Coober Pedy are miners. Miners **dig** under the ground. They go down very **deep** to **look for** gold or special stones. Coober Pedy is famous for opals. Opals are beautiful white stones. People put opals in jewelry.

2   Miners **discovered** opals in Coober Pedy in 1915. At that time, many miners lived in simple **holes** under the ground. Aboriginal people laughed at them. The Aboriginal people are the **native** people of Australia. They called the area *kupa piti*. This means "white man in a hole" in their language.

3   Today, Coober Pedy has about 2,000 people living in underground homes. And the town also has underground restaurants, hotels, and churches. It is like other towns. But the people don't have a **view**. A new underground house with five rooms costs about $25,000. Some homes even have swimming pools!

4   The people of Coober Pedy live underground for several reasons. One reason is there are no trees around the town. The last tree died in 1971. People need wood from trees to build houses. But the **main** reason why people live under the ground is the very hot weather. The temperature in the summer goes up to 122°F (50°C). Under the ground, the temperature always stays the same: 77°F (25°C).

5   Thousands of years ago, the people of Cappadocia, in Turkey, dug hundreds of underground cities. They used these cities as **hiding places** when enemies attacked them. The largest of these underground cities had eleven floors. It could shelter as many as 50,000 people for several months. Today, some people live underground in Cappadocia, but it is by choice. They are not hiding from anybody!

6   **In the future**, more people will live under the ground. They will have different reasons. Japan, for instance, wants to build a city under the ground because it has a lot of people and little land. The name of the city will be Alice City. About 100,000 people will live there. It will have offices, hotels, sports centers, and theaters. To **design** an underground city is very interesting, **of course**. But can people really live with no sun and no sky?

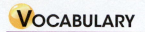

VOCABULARY

MEANING

Write the correct words in the blanks.

deep	dig	holes	native
design	discovered	main	view

1. Miners make holes in the ground. They _____ in the ground.

2. Miners work far down under the ground. They work _____ under the ground.

3. In 1915, miners _____ opals in Coober Pedy. They found opals.

4. The Aboriginal people were born in Australia. They are the _____ people of Australia.

5. There are many reasons why people live underground. The weather is the most important reason. It is the _____ reason.

6. They can't see things outside. They do not have a _____.

7. The people live in openings in the ground. They live in _____.

8. It is interesting for an architect to _____ an underground city.

WORDS THAT GO TOGETHER

Write the correct words in the blanks.

hiding places	in the future	look for	of course

1. More people will live underground in twenty or thirty years. They will live underground _____.

2. Miners try to find many things underground. They _____ gold or special stones.

3. I am not surprised that people like to live underground. It is an interesting place to live. _____, people like to live there.

4. In the past, the people of Cappadocia used the underground cities as _____ from their enemies. They did not want their enemies to find them.

USE

Work with a partner to answer the questions. Use complete sentences.

1. What animal likes to *dig*?
2. What is the *main* reason you want to learn English?
3. What is the *view* from your classroom windows?
4. What are some reasons people dig *holes* in the ground?
5. Why do people go in *deep* water?
6. What do you want to do *in the future*?

COMPREHENSION

UNDERSTANDING THE READING

Circle the letter of the correct answer.

1. People in Coober Pedy live under the ground because _____.

    a. it costs $25,000   b. they have trees   c. it is not hot there

2. The people of Cappadocia used their underground cities to _____.

    a. look for gold   b. hide from enemies   c. live

3. Japan is planning an underground city because _____.

    a. it has a lot of people   b. it has a lot of enemies   c. the weather is very hot
    and little land

REMEMBERING DETAILS

Reread the passage and answer the questions.

1. Where is Coober Pedy?
2. How many people live underground in Coober Pedy?
3. What are the native people of Australia called?
4. Where is Cappadocia?
5. How many people could find shelter in the largest underground city in Cappadocia?
6. What is the name of the underground city Japan is planning to build?

SENTENCE COMPLETION

Match the words in column A and column B to make sentences.

A	B
____ **1.** Coober Pedy is	**a.** as hiding places.
____ **2.** Japan has	**b.** a view.
____ **3.** The people used these underground cities	**c.** homes and restaurants.
	d. a lot of people and little land.
____ **4.** Coober Pedy has	**e.** under the ground for valuable things.
____ **5.** Underground homes don't have	**f.** very hot above the ground.
____ **6.** Miners dig	

DICTATION

Work with a partner. Read three sentences from the exercise above. Your partner listens and writes the sentences. Then your partner reads three sentences and you write them.

DISCUSSION

Discuss the answers to these questions with your classmates.

1. Would you like to live underground? What would be the best thing? What would be the worst thing?
2. What do you think about Japan's underground city?
3. Where are some other unusual places people live?

CRITICAL THINKING

Work with a partner. Ask each other the following questions. Discuss your answers.

1. Imagine you are living in a perfect place for you. Where are you? What kind of house are you living in? What is the weather like there? What grows there? Is it peaceful? What view do you have from your window?
2. The Japanese want to build a city of the future under the ground. What is your idea of a city of the future? What would it look like? How many people would live there? What name would you give it?

WRITING

Complete the sentences about people who live under the ground.

EXAMPLE   People live under the ground in *Coober Pedy*_____.

1. Miners dig _____.

2. Coober Pedy has _____.

3. One reason people live underground _____.

4. The main reason is _____.

5. In the future, _____.

SPELLING AND PUNCTUATION

EXCLAMATION POINTS

We use an **exclamation point** at the end of a sentence to show **strong emotion** (feeling or excitement) or a **strong command**. An exclamation point makes the words stronger and louder.

Some homes have swimming pools!
Ken! Come here!

We do **NOT use a period** before or after an exclamation point.

*Write **C** for sentences with correct punctuation. Rewrite the incorrect sentences. Use exclamation points for incorrect periods. Use periods for incorrect exclamation points.*

_____ 1. Look. There's a man in the hole. _____

_____ 2. What a great idea. _____

_____ 3. Wow. There are no trees in the town. _____

_____ 4. Coober Pedy is a town in South Australia!. _____

_____ 5. Miners work under the ground. _____

_____ 6. The miners found thousands of opals!. _____

 Go to page 139 for the Internet Activity.

Go to page 139 for the Internet Activity.

DID YOU KNOW?	• In Andalucia, Spain, thousands of houses carved out of caves hundreds of years ago are today modernized with all the amenities. You can buy or rent them. • Underground homes have a comfortable temperature all year round.	

WHY DO PEOPLE DECORATE THEIR BODIES?

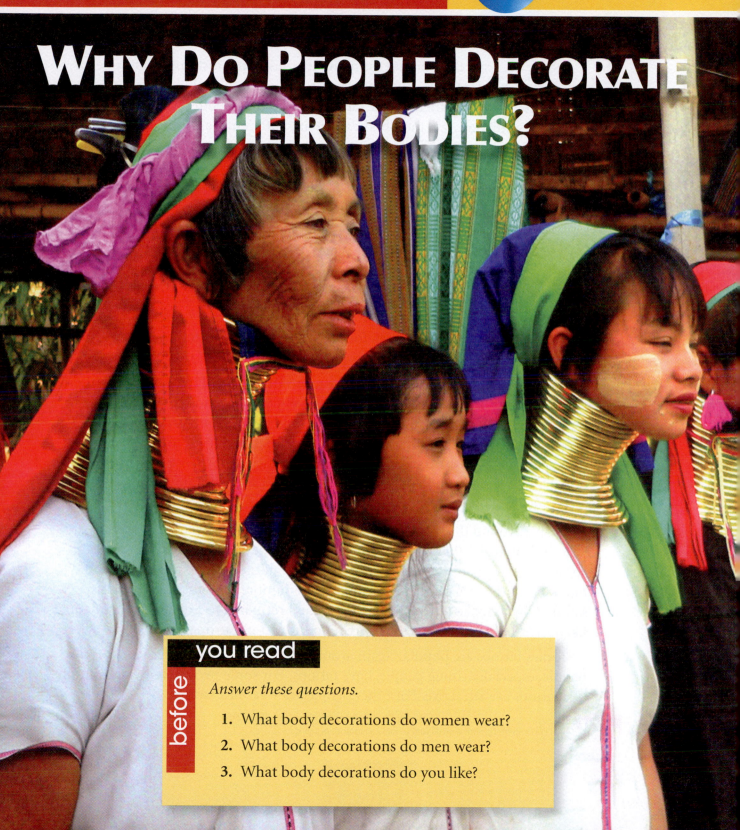

before **you read**

Answer these questions.

1. What body decorations do women wear?
2. What body decorations do men wear?
3. What body decorations do you like?

WHY DO PEOPLE DECORATE THEIR BODIES?

1   People decorate their bodies for many reasons. The most important one, of course, is to be **attractive**. Another one is to show that they **belong to** a group. For one reason or another, people have decorated their bodies for thousands of years. They still decorate their bodies in many different ways.

2   Some people decorate their **lips**, ears, and necks to look beautiful. For example, in Africa, the Surmese women wear a plate in their bottom lips. How do they do this? First, a mother makes a hole in her daughter's bottom lip. Then she **stretches** the lip. Then she **puts** a small plate **in** it. As the daughter gets older, she puts in bigger and bigger plates. Other people in Africa put plates in their ears. They want the bottom of their ears to hang to their shoulders.

3   The Kayan women of Burma (Myanmar) are called *long-necked women*. These women wear metal neck rings to stretch their necks. They wear more rings as they get older. Their necks become longer—sometimes two or three times the **normal** size. Most Kayan women follow this tradition. But today, some of the younger women break the tradition and **take off** their neck rings.

4   People also decorate their teeth to be more attractive. Many Americans and Europeans like **straight** white teeth. They spend a lot of money to fix and clean their teeth. This is not true in other parts of the world. In east Africa, some people **pull out** their bottom teeth. They want their top teeth to **stick out**. In some parts of Asia, the tradition was for women to paint their teeth black. Today, only older women still do this. In Indonesia, boys and girls file[1] their teeth. A person with filed teeth will have a good and healthy life.

5   People around the world always liked tattoos. Europeans learned about tattoos around 1770. A famous English explorer named Captain Cook went to Tahiti. He saw people there with tattoos. The Tahitians called the decoration *tatou*. From this, we get the word *tattoo*. The Tahitians taught Cook and his sailors how to make tattoos. When the sailors **returned** to England, other people liked their tattoos. Soon tattoos **spread** to the rest of Europe.

6   Today, tattoos are popular again around the world. Many different types of people, especially young people, have tattoos. For some people, body decorations like tattoos are attractive. For other people, they are just strange.

---

[1] **file**: to rub something with a metal tool to make it smooth or cut it

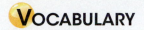

MEANING

Write the correct words in the blanks.

| attractive | normal | spread | stretches |
| lips | returned | straight | |

1. The women's necks are longer than the usual size. They are longer than the _____ size.

2. In Africa, a group of women like plates in their _____. The plate is on the outside edge of the mouth.

3. Some women decorate their bodies to be beautiful. They want to be _____.

4. The sailors went back to their homes. They _____ home.

5. Her teeth are _____. They are regular and in a perfect line.

6. The mother pulls her daughter's lip. She wants the lip to be longer. She _____ it.

7. People all over Europe learned about tattoos. Tattoos _____ from England to the rest of Europe.

WORDS THAT GO TOGETHER

Write the correct words in the blanks.

| belong to | pull out | puts in | stick out | take off |

1. Many people want to _____ a group. They want to be together with other people.

2. He can't close his mouth. His teeth _____.

3. She has very bad teeth. The dentist had to _____ three of them.

4. The woman makes a hole in her ear. Then she _____ a small earring.

5. The woman is wearing neck rings. When she wants to break the tradition, she will _____ the rings.

USE

Work with a partner to answer the questions. Use complete sentences.

1. What do many women put in their *lips*?
2. What part of your body do you *stretch*?
3. What time do you *return* home after school or work?
4. What is a *normal* breakfast for you?
5. What group (or groups) do you *belong to*?
6. What body decorations are *attractive* to you?

COMPREHENSION

UNDERSTANDING THE READING

Circle the letter of the correct answer.

1. In Africa, they decorate their lips and ears to look _____.

   a. strange   **b.** beautiful   **c.** rich

2. Sailors learned about tattoos in _____.

   a. Burma   **b.** Europe   **c.** Tahiti

3. Today, many different types of people _____.

   a. want black teeth   **b.** have tattoos   **c.** have long necks

REMEMBERING DETAILS

Reread the passage and answer the questions.

1. What do some women in Africa put in their ears?
2. Why are the Kayan women called *long-necked women*?
3. In what part of the world do some people pull out their bottom teeth?
4. What do some women in Asia do to their teeth?
5. Who was Captain Cook?
6. Where did Captain Cook see tattoos?

SENTENCE COMPLETION

Match the words in column A and column B to make sentences.

A	B
____ **1.** Many Americans and Europeans like	**a.** their teeth black.
____ **2.** Some women in Burma stretch	**b.** their bodies for many reasons.
____ **3.** Some women in Asia paint	**c.** show they belong to a group.
____ **4.** People decorate	**d.** white teeth.
____ **5.** Some people have tattoos to	**e.** the rest of Europe.
____ **6.** Tattoos spread from England to	**f.** their necks.

DICTATION

Work with a partner. Read three sentences from the exercise above. Your partner listens and writes the sentences. Then your partner reads three sentences and you write them.

DISCUSSION

Discuss the answers to these questions with your classmates.

1. What body decoration is popular in your country?
2. What body decoration do you want to have?
3. What are other ways to decorate the body?

CRITICAL THINKING

Work with a partner. Ask each other the following questions. Discuss your answers.

1. Huge lips are beautiful to the Surmese. Long necks are beautiful to the Kayans. What does this tell us about beauty? Where do we get our ideas about beauty? What makes a man or a woman beautiful in your culture?

2. People like to decorate themselves like others in their group. They wear similar hairstyles and body decorations. Why do people want to look like others? What happens to people who look different from others in their group? Is looking like others important to you? Why or why not?

WRITING

Complete the sentences about body decoration.

EXAMPLE   People decorate their bodies *to be attractive*   .

1. In Africa, some women _____ .

2. In Burma, some women _____ .

3. In east Africa, some people _____ .

4. In Asia, some women _____ .

5. Today, tattoos _____ .

SPELLING AND PUNCTUATION

PLURALS: NOUNS ENDING IN -O

Some singular nouns end in *-o*. To make these nouns **plural**, look at the **letter before the -*o*.**

- If the letter is a **vowel**, add *-s*.
  tattoo—tattoos   video—videos

- If the letter is a **consonant**, add *-es*.
  hero—heroes   potato—potatoes

Some words have **special rules**.
  kilo—kilos   photo—photos   piano—pianos   solo—solos

Underline the misspelled words. Write the correct words on the lines.

1. The lead singer of the group has tattooes.   _____

2. His hair is very red. It looks like tomatos.   _____

3. The group has many videoes.   _____

4. They have crazy hair, but they are my heros.   _____

5. I have a lot of photoes of them on my walls.   _____

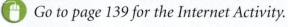 *Go to page 139 for the Internet Activity.*

 DID YOU KNOW?
- **A 5,300-year-old mummy was found with tattoos! (Otzi the Iceman)**
- **In India and Morocco, women make designs on their bodies with a (plant) coloring called henna.**

WHO ARE THE UROS?

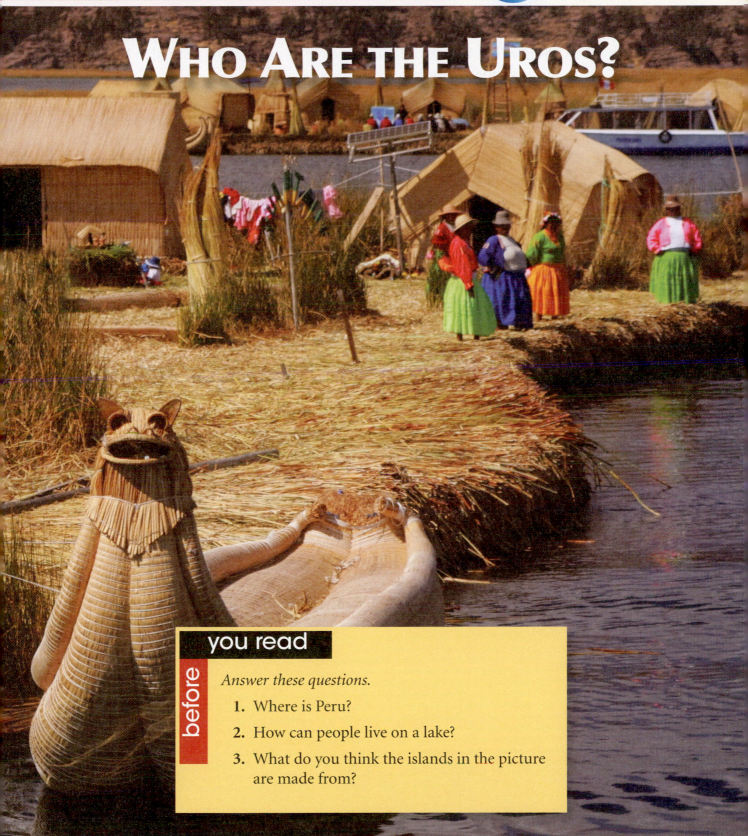

before you read

Answer these questions.

1. Where is Peru?

2. How can people live on a lake?

3. What do you think the islands in the picture are made from?

WHO ARE THE UROS?

1   The Uros are a very old Indian **tribe** that lives on **Lake** Titicaca, in Peru. Lake Titicaca is one of the highest lakes in the world. It is 12,500 feet above sea level. The Uros have lived there for hundreds of years on small floating islands. They make these islands themselves.

2   The Uros use totora reeds to make their floating islands. Totora reeds are tall plants that grow in the lake. The Uros **tie** the reeds together to make **rafts**. These are about 4 to 8 feet thick. When the reeds get soft, the Uros must put new ones on top. These islands last for about thirty years. Then they make new ones. There are forty-two of these islands on the lake. Each island is home to several families. The larger islands have about ten families. The smaller islands have two or three families that live on them. Their houses, their furniture, and their boats are made of totora reeds as well.

3   The Uros have many other uses for the totora reed. One important use is for food. For instance, they eat the **tender** bottom of the plant. They also make a flour from the totora, and they use it to make bread. They even make tea from its flowers. Another important use is for medicine. To take away pain, they **wrap** the plant around the place where they have pain. Finally, when they need a change from the totora plant, they take it to the **mainland** and exchange it to get other foods or medicines they need.

4   The Uros have a very traditional way of life. The men go fishing and hunt birds. The women cook on a fire over **a pile of** stones. This way they do not **burn** the totora under it. The women also make and sell **handicrafts** to tourists.

5   The Uros like **modern technology**, too. Some boats have motors. Some houses have **solar panels**, and they have televisions. The main island has a radio station, and it plays music for several hours a day.

6   Sadly, more and more young Uros are going to the **mainland** for jobs. The number of Uros who live on the islands may get smaller. In that case, the Uros and their traditional way of life could disappear.

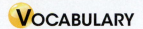

VOCABULARY

MEANING

Write the correct words in the blanks.

burn	lake	rafts	tie	wrap
handicrafts	mainland	tender	tribe	

1. They put the reeds side by side and _____ or attach them together.

2. They make _____, or platforms that float with the totora reeds.

3. They do not eat the hard part of the plant; they eat the _____ part.

4. They _____, or cover the place where they have pain with a piece of the totora plant.

5. He lives with his _____. They are all related. The chief is one of his great-uncles.

6. There are no jobs on the islands. They are too small. To get a job, you have to go to the _____.

7. The Uro women sell _____, or traditional things they make by hand.

8. Titicaca is a _____, or a large area of water with land all around it.

9. When they make a fire, they must be careful not to _____ the totora reeds under it.

WORDS THAT GO TOGETHER

Write the correct words in the blanks.

a pile of	modern technology	solar panels

1. They have _____, or machines such as televisions, radios, and motor boats.

2. The houses have _____ to get electricity from the sun.

3. They make _____ stones and make a fire on it. This way, it does not burn the totora.

USE

Work with a partner to answer the questions. Use complete sentences.

1. What vegetable is good when it is *tender*?
2. What is something you *tie*?
3. What do you do when you *burn* yourself?
4. What is the name of a *lake* you know?
5. Why do people have *solar panels*?
6. What is the best invention in *modern technology* for you?

COMPREHENSION

UNDERSTANDING THE READING

Circle the letter of the correct answer.

1. The islands that the Uros live on _____.

   a. last forever
   b. are different sizes
   c. never move

2. The Uros _____.

   a. use the totora plant in many ways
   b. don't allow visitors to their islands
   c. often burn the totora when they cook food

3. The Uros have _____.

   a. no contact with the outside world
   b. a traditional way of life with some modern machines
   c. a modern way of life with lots of technology

REMEMBERING DETAILS

*Circle **T** if the sentence is true. Circle **F** if the sentence is false.*

1. Lake Titicaca is one of the highest lakes in the world.   T   F

2. The totora plant grows outside the lake.   T   F

3. Each island has one family living on it.   T   F

4. The Uros use totora reeds to make houses and boats.   T   F

5. When the Uros want to eat something different, they plant new crops.   T   F

6. Many young Uros leave to get jobs on the mainland.   T   F

SENTENCE COMPLETION

Match the words in column A and column B to make sentences.

A	B
____ 1. The Uros live	**a.** with the totora.
____ 2. They use the totora	**b.** floating islands.
____ 3. They make floating islands	**c.** on Lake Titicaca.
____ 4. There are forty-two	**d.** for many things.
____ 5. The women sell	**e.** the mainland for jobs.
____ 6. Young Uros are going to	**f.** handicrafts to tourists.

DICTATION

Work with a partner. Read three sentences from the exercise above. Your partner listens and writes the sentences. Then your partner reads three sentences and you write them.

DISCUSSION

Discuss the answers to these questions with your classmates.

1. Are there people in your country who still have a traditional way of life? Who are they? Where and how do they live?
2. Each country has its own way of treating health problems or its own traditional medicine. What is the traditional medicine in your country for an upset stomach, a headache, or a cold?
3. Would you like to live on a small island like the Uros? Why or why not?

CRITICAL THINKING

Work with a partner. Ask each other the following questions. Discuss your answers.

1. Many traditional cultures are disappearing today. What are the reasons why? Do you think it is important to keep traditional ways of life?
2. What are the advantages of living in a modern society? What are the disadvantages? What are the advantages and disadvantages of having a traditional way of life? Which type of life do you like better? Why?

WRITING

Complete the sentences about the Uros.

EXAMPLE   The Uros live   *on small floating islands*   .

1. The islands are on _____.

2. The Uros use _____.

3. The plant grows _____.

4. The women _____.

5. Young Uros _____.

SPELLING AND PUNCTUATION

CAPITAL LETTERS: GEOGRAPHICAL NAMES

> We use a **capital letter** for **names of geographical places**, such as lakes, mountains, deserts, seas, oceans, rivers, and gulfs. We do **NOT** use a capital letter for *the* or *of* in the name.
>
> *They live on Lake Titicaca.*
>
> We do **NOT** use a capital letter for a **place with no special name**.
>
> *They live on a lake.*

Underline and correct the words that need capital letters. Remember the capital letter rules from other units.

1. The amazon river is in south america.

2. There are many islands on lake titicaca.

3. The highest waterfall is angel falls in venezuela.

4. Some seas have names of colors, like the black sea and the red sea.

5. The biggest lake in africa is lake victoria.

Go to page 140 for the Internet Activity.

Go to page 140 for the Internet Activity.

| **DID YOU KNOW?** | • The Ma'dan Marsh Arabs live in marshes in Iraq. They live much like the Uros on islands made of reeds.
 • The World is a group of 300 man-made islands in Dubai. It looks like a map of the world. | |

WHAT IS CANADA'S FAVORITE SPORT?

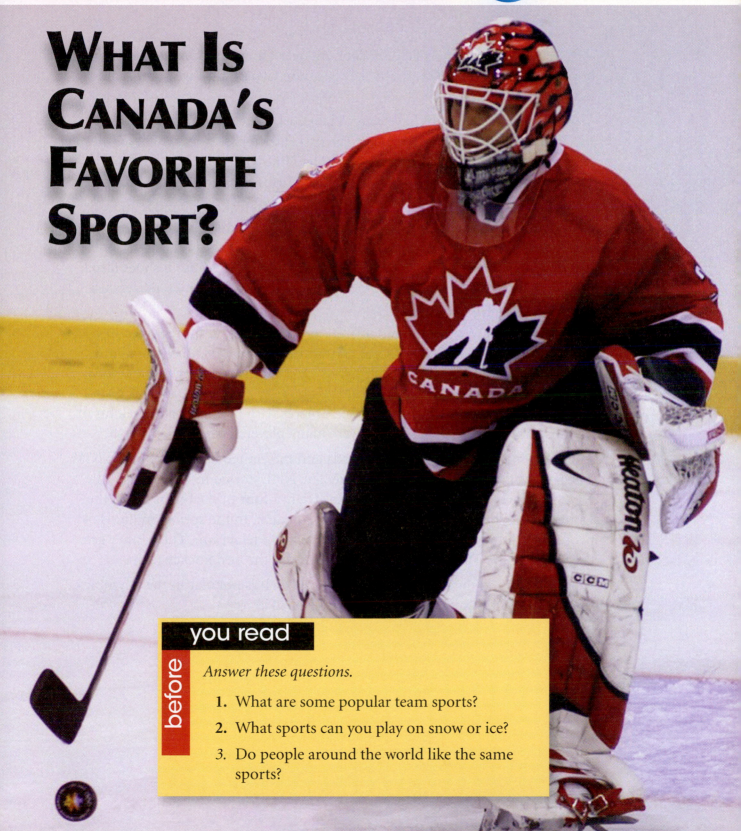

before you read

Answer these questions.

1. What are some popular team sports?

2. What sports can you play on snow or ice?

3. Do people around the world like the same sports?

WHAT IS CANADA'S FAVORITE SPORT?

1   Canada's favorite sport is ice hockey. All over Canada today, men, women, boys, and girls play hockey. Ice hockey began in Canada, but we do not know exactly how it began.

2   **At first**, hockey did not have rules. Then, in 1880, Canadian students at McGill University in Montreal made the first rules for ice hockey. These rules changed in 1911 and 1912. The new rules had lines on the ice to make special areas. There were also six players on a **team**. This is **similar to** hockey today.

3   Ice hockey is the world's fastest sport. Players often **skate** 30 miles an hour. They get tired quickly. Often, hockey players leave a **game** and other players come in. In hockey, players use a stick to hit a puck. A puck is like a ball, but it is **flat**. It **slides** on the ice. It is better to use a cold puck because it slides faster. Players put the puck in the freezer before a game. In some games, players use more than thirty pucks!

4   Hockey looks easy to play, but it isn't easy. Players try to hit the puck into the other team's **goal**. The puck goes faster than the players. Pucks go about 100 miles an hour. Hockey is a dangerous sport. Many players **get hurt**. Today, players wear special clothes to protect their bodies. The player near the goal wears a mask to protect his or her face. A player with no mask can break his or her nose or teeth. In the past, there were many players with no front teeth.

5   **Professional** hockey teams in Canada and the United States play in the NHL. This means the *National Hockey League*. The NHL started in 1917. Today, the NHL has thirty teams in North America. Twenty-four of the teams are in the United States, but most of the players are Canadian. In the spring, millions of people watch the **final** hockey game of the year on television. The winner gets the Stanley Cup. The Stanley Cup is the **prize** for the best hockey team.

6   People around the world play ice hockey now. It is popular in the Olympics. But hockey will always be Canada's special sport.

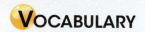

VOCABULARY

MEANING

Write the correct words in the blanks.

final	game	prize	skate	team
flat	goal	professional	slides	

1. Hockey players do not walk on the ice. They wear special shoes to

    _____ on the ice.

2. The puck moves smoothly on the ice. It _____.

3. People do not play hockey alone. They play hockey on a _____ with

    other people.

4. The two teams played against each other last night. I saw the _____

    on television.

5. There are many hockey games in the year. The last game is called the

    _____ game.

6. The best hockey team gets the Stanley Cup. This is the greatest _____.

7. A hockey puck is _____. It is smooth. It is not like a ball.

8. Hockey is a dangerous sport. The player near the _____ has to wear

    a mask to protect his or her face.

9. Players in the NHL get money to play. It is their job to play hockey. They are

    _____ players.

WORDS THAT GO TOGETHER

Write the correct words in the blanks.

at first	get hurt	similar to

1. In the beginning, hockey didn't have rules. Today, hockey has rules.

    _____, hockey was different from hockey today.

2. Ice hockey in 1911 was about the same as hockey today. They are

    _____ each other.

3. Hockey players sometimes fall and break bones. They _____.

USE

Work with a partner to answer the questions. Use complete sentences.

1. What sports *team* do you like?
2. What is a famous *prize* in sports?
3. What sport is football *similar to*?
4. When do you *slide*?
5. What is something that is *flat*?
6. What do you do when you *get hurt*?

COMPREHENSION

UNDERSTANDING THE READING

Circle the letter of the correct answer.

1. Ice hockey is _____.

   a. the world's easiest sport

   b. the world's fastest sport

   c. the world's newest sport

2. The NHL _____.

   a. has thirty teams in North America

   b. started in 1911

   c. does not play in the spring

3. Players change during a game because _____.

   a. they get cold

   b. they need a new puck

   c. they get tired

REMEMBERING DETAILS

Reread the passage and answer the questions.

1. Who made the first rules for ice hockey?
2. How many players are on a hockey team?
3. How fast do players go?
4. What do players hit with a stick?
5. Why do players wear special clothes?
6. What is the name of the prize the best hockey team gets?

SENTENCE COMPLETION

Match the words in column A and column B to make sentences.

A	B
_____ 1. A puck	**a.** play hockey.
_____ 2. Players wear	**b.** a dangerous sport.
_____ 3. Canadian students	**c.** slides on the ice.
_____ 4. Hockey began	**d.** special clothes to protect their bodies.
_____ 5. Hockey is	**e.** made the first rules for hockey.
_____ 6. People around the world	**f.** in Canada.

DICTATION

Work with a partner. Read three sentences from the exercise above. Your partner listens and writes the sentences. Then your partner reads three sentences and you write them.

DISCUSSION

Discuss the answers to these questions with your classmates.

1. What is your favorite team sport?
2. What is the most popular sport in your country?
3. Do you play any sports? Which ones?

CRITICAL THINKING

Work with a partner. Ask each other the following questions. Discuss your answers.

1. Do sports have a great importance to the people of your country? Why or why not? How are sports good for a country? Are sports ever bad for countries or individuals? What good have the Olympics done in the world?
2. Ice hockey started in the cold and snowy climate of Canada. Name some sports that began in places because of their climate or geography. How do climate, geography, and people have an influence on what sports are played and are popular in a country or region?

WRITING

Complete the sentences about ice hockey.

EXAMPLE   Ice hockey is <u>*Canada's favorite sport*</u>   .

1. Ice hockey is _____.

2. Players wear _____.

3. Players use _____.

4. Professional hockey teams _____.

5. The Stanley Cup is _____.

SPELLING AND PUNCTUATION

APOSTROPHES: POSSESSION

We use an apostrophe (') or an apostrophe + *s* ('s) to **show possession with nouns**.

Singular noun NOT ending in -*s*: **'s**	*Canada's favorite sport is ice hockey.*
Singular noun ending in -*s*: **'** or **'s**	*Chris' brother plays for the NHL.*
	Chris's brother plays for the NHL.
Plural noun NOT ending in -*s*: **'s**	*The women's games are dangerous, too.*
Plural noun ending in -*s*: **'**	*The players' sticks are new.*

Underline the words that need apostrophes. Write the correct words on the lines.

1. The worlds fastest sport is hockey.   _____

2. The professional players salaries are high.   _____

3. The childrens favorite sport is hockey.   _____

4. James shot was great.   _____

5. The players skate is broken.   _____

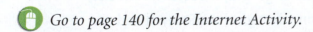 *Go to page 140 for the Internet Activity.*

Go to page 140 for the Internet Activity.

DID YOU KNOW?	• Other types of hockey that are not popular in Canada but are popular in other parts of the world: field hockey and roller skate hockey. • Women's ice hockey was played for the first time at the Olympics in 1998.	

WHAT'S SPECIAL ABOUT NEW ZEALAND?

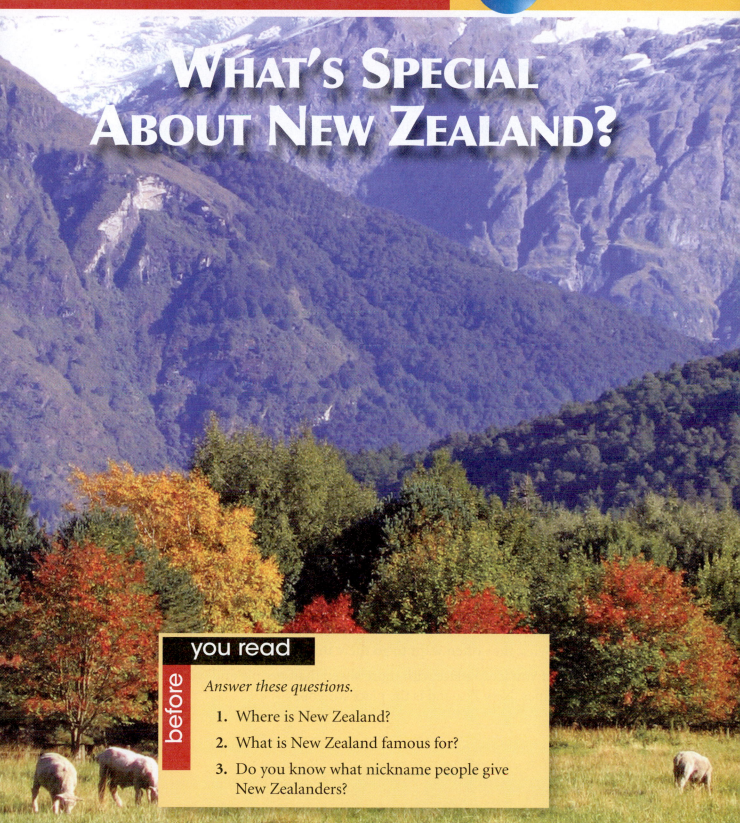

before you read

Answer these questions.

1. Where is New Zealand?

2. What is New Zealand famous for?

3. Do you know what nickname people give New Zealanders?

WHAT'S SPECIAL ABOUT NEW ZEALAND?

1   It has more sheep than people! It has a population of 40 million sheep and 4 million people. This means there are ten sheep for every human being in New Zealand. New Zealand's size is about the same as Great Britain, Japan, or Colorado. So, with its small human population, it is one of the world's least **crowded** countries.

2   The country is **made up of** two islands: North Island and South Island. There are also some smaller islands. Most of the people live on the North Island. For a country with so few people, it is **civilized**. The capital, Wellington, has more cafés and restaurants **per person** than New York City. New Zealand also has more **golf courses** per person than any other country.

3   Most of the people of New Zealand are of European **origin**. The native people of New Zealand, the Maori, make up 14 percent of the population. They have their own language and culture. Some Maori words are very long and difficult to say. Try pronouncing this Maori name for one of the **hills** of the North Island: *Taumatawhakatangihangakoauauotamateaturipukakapikimaungahoronukupokai whenuakitanatahu*. It is the longest place name in the world.

4   New Zealand is **isolated** from the outside world, so its plants and animals are unique. About 80 percent of New Zealand's plants only grow in New Zealand. Before humans came, there were no land animals. Even today, there are no snakes in New Zealand. Several kinds of birds have no animals to be afraid of. Now they have become land birds and cannot fly. One example of this is the kiwi. This native bird of New Zealand is the symbol of New Zealand. New Zealanders are often called *kiwis* **in slang**.

5   The country is famous for its **spectacular** natural beauty. It has huge mountains and volcanoes, long sandy **beaches**, subtropical forests, and green **countryside**. Because of its beauty, New Zealand has become popular with moviemakers. Many movies, such as *Jurassic Park 2, The Lord of the Rings* trilogy, and *The Lion, the Witch, and the Wardrobe*, were filmed there. After people watch the movies, they often want to go there themselves.

6   So, if you like a place with more sheep than people and with spectacular landscapes, New Zealand is the place for you!

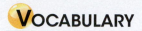

VOCABULARY

MEANING

Write the correct words in the blanks.

| beaches | countryside | hills | origin |
| civilized | crowded | isolated | spectacular |

1. New Zealand has a lot of land and few people. It's not a(n) _____ country.

2. New Zealand is far from other countries. It is _____.

3. New Zealand is amazing, or _____ in its natural beauty.

4. Outside the cities and towns, the _____ is green and beautiful.

5. By the ocean, the long sandy _____ are great for swimmers.

6. The big cities in New Zealand have restaurants, stores, and theaters, just like other big cities. They are _____.

7. Most people in New Zealand come from Europe. They are of European _____.

8. There are mountains, and there are also smaller _____. One of them has a very long name.

WORDS THAT GO TOGETHER

Write the correct words in the blanks.

| golf courses | in slang | made up of | per person |

1. Other people call the people of New Zealand "kiwis" _____.

2. People play golf on _____.

3. New Zealand is _____ two islands.

4. For each person, or _____, there are more restaurants than in New York City.

USE

Work with a partner to answer the questions. Use complete sentences.

1. Where are there nice *beaches* in your country or a place you know?
2. What is your family's *origin*?
3. Why do people visit the *countryside*?
4. Do you know a city that is very *crowded*? What is its name?
5. What is a *spectacular* place to visit?
6. What other country in the world is *isolated*?

COMPREHENSION

UNDERSTANDING THE READING

Circle the letter of the correct answer.

1. New Zealand has _____.

   a. more cafés than sheep
   b. no modern cities
   c. both culture and natural beauty

2. Many of New Zealand's plants and animals are unique because _____.

   a. New Zealand is far away from the rest of the world
   b. Europeans brought them from other parts of the world
   c. there were no land animals before humans came

3. New Zealand is famous for its _____.

   a. movies
   b. natural landscape
   c. restaurants

REMEMBERING DETAILS

Reread the passage and answer the questions.

1. What is the size of New Zealand?
2. What is the capital?
3. Who are the native people of New Zealand?
4. What animal does not exist in New Zealand?
5. What kinds of birds live in New Zealand?
6. Why is New Zealand popular with moviemakers?

SENTENCE COMPLETION

Match the words in column A and column B to make sentences.

A		B
_____ **1.** There are a lot of sheep		**a.** are unique.
_____ **2.** New Zealand's plants and animals		**b.** snakes in New Zealand.
_____ **3.** There are no		**c.** in New Zealand.
_____ **4.** The symbol of New Zealand is		**d.** kiwis.
_____ **5.** People call New Zealanders		**e.** and cannot fly.
_____ **6.** The kiwi is a land bird		**f.** the kiwi.

DICTATION

Work with a partner. Read three sentences from the exercise above. Your partner listens and writes the sentences. Then your partner reads three sentences and you write them.

DISCUSSION

Discuss the answers to these questions with your classmates.

1. Do you like sports and the outdoors, or do you like culture and cities? Would you like to travel to New Zealand? Why or why not?

2. Does your country have a large or small population? Would you like to live in a place that has more animals than people? Why or why not?

3. What size is your country? What kind of landscapes does it have? What is the most beautiful area?

CRITICAL THINKING

Work with a partner. Ask each other the following questions. Discuss your answers.

1. What is your country most famous for? What is special about your country? What are you most proud of? Is your country a nice place for people to visit? Why or why not?

2. In New Zealand, there are Maoris and also people of different European origins. How important is it to have people of different origins in the same country? How does it affect the culture of a country? What are its good sides and bad sides?

WRITING

Complete the sentences about New Zealand.

EXAMPLE   New Zealand has   *a population of 40 million sheep and 4 million people* .

1. The native people _____.

2. The plants and animals _____.

3. New Zealanders are called _____.

4. New Zealand is famous _____.

5. New Zealand is popular _____.

SPELLING AND PUNCTUATION

CAPITAL LETTERS: TITLES OF WORKS

> We use **capital letters** for the **titles** of **movies**, **songs**, and **books**. We begin the following words with capital letters:
>
> - the first word
> - the last word
> - all important words (nouns, pronouns, verbs, adjectives, and adverbs)
> - all prepositions of five letters or more
>
> *The Lord of the Rings*   *Here Comes the Sun*   *A Tale of Two Cities*

Rewrite the following titles of movies made in New Zealand with the correct capital letters.

1. the last samurai   _____

2. the chronicles of narnia   _____

3. an angel at my table   _____

4. the world's fastest indian   _____

5. the return of the king   _____

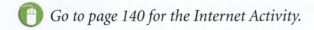 *Go to page 140 for the Internet Activity.*

DID YOU KNOW ?	• New Zealand was the first democracy in the West to give women the right to vote. • Edmund Hilary, the first person to climb Mt. Everest, was born in New Zealand.	

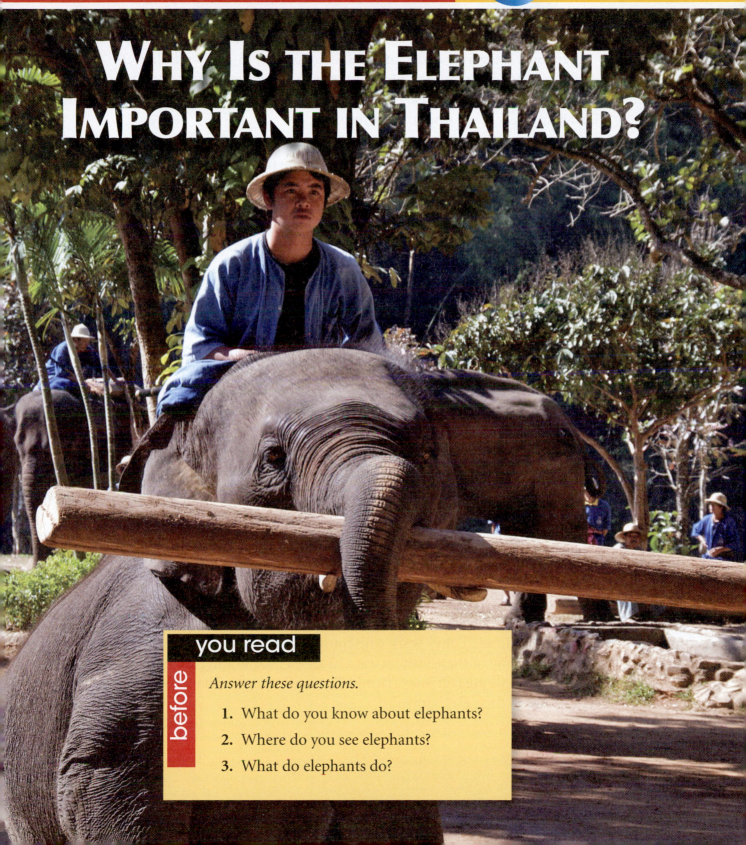

WHY IS THE ELEPHANT IMPORTANT IN THAILAND?

before you read

Answer these questions.

1. What do you know about elephants?
2. Where do you see elephants?
3. What do elephants do?

WHY IS THE ELEPHANT IMPORTANT IN THAILAND?

1   Elephants are strong and **gentle** at the same time. In Thailand, they are symbols of **power** and peace. Elephants are also a very important part of Thailand's history. Many years ago, they did important work: They helped the Thai people get wood from their forests.

2   Today, the Thai people want to keep the trees in their forests. They **cut down** only a few trees. Some elephants still work in the forests because the forests are in the mountains. Trucks and machines cannot go up the mountains, but elephants can. Men cut down the trees, and the elephants pick up the trees. Then the elephants **carry** the trees to the river. The trees **float** down the river to other men. The men cut the trees into pieces of wood.

3   In the past, the Thai people cut down a lot of trees. They needed a lot of elephants to work in the forests to help them. Special people **trained** the elephants for many years to teach them to do this work. Each elephant had its own trainer, or *mahout*. A *mahout* **spent his life** with the same elephant. Fathers wanted their sons to be *mahouts*, too. *Mahouts* bought baby elephants for their sons. First, the baby elephant stayed with its mother. When the elephant was three years old, it lived with the boy. The boy and the elephant grew up together. The boy took care of the elephant. They learned a lot about each other.

4   A *mahout* trained, fed, and took care of his elephant. This was a difficult job. An elephant eats 550 pounds (250 kilos) of plants and drinks 80 gallons (300 liters) of water every day! It trained every day for six hours. The elephant **got used to** the *mahout*. It remembered the *mahout's* **voice** and smell. It understood its *mahout's* **instructions** and obeyed him. It did not obey other *mahouts*. The *mahout* trained the elephant for twenty years. At age twenty, the elephant began to work. Elephants worked for about thirty-five years. They stopped work at age fifty-five or sixty—like people.

5   Today, some elephants and *mahouts* still do this type of work, but most of them do not. Instead, they work with tourists. Millions of people visit Thailand every year. Many of these visitors want to see elephants and take rides on them. So, the elephants are still important in Thailand, and the Thai people are still very **proud of** their elephants.

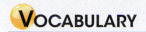

MEANING

Write the correct words in the blanks.

carry	gentle	power	voice
float	instructions	trained	

1. The elephant is a _____ animal. It is very nice. It doesn't hurt people.

2. The trees lay in the water. They stay on top of the water. The trees _____.

3. The elephants hold the trees and take them to another place. They _____ the trees.

4. In Thailand, people _____ elephants. They taught them to do work.

5. The elephant is a symbol of _____. It is very big and strong.

6. The *mahout* speaks in a certain way. The elephant knows how the *mahout* sounds. The elephant knows its *mahout's* _____.

7. The *mahout* says to do something. Then the elephant does it. The elephant listens to the *mahout's* _____.

WORDS THAT GO TOGETHER

Write the correct words in the blanks.

cut down	got used to	proud of	spent his life

1. The *mahout* was with the elephant every day. He _____ with the elephant.

2. The Thai people are happy about their elephants. They think the elephants are good. The Thai people are _____ them.

3. The men want the tree to fall to the ground. They use a big knife or a machine. The men _____ the tree.

4. The *mahouts* and the elephants knew each other very well. They became good friends. They _____ each other.

USE

Work with a partner to answer the questions. Use complete sentences.

1. Who are you *proud of*?
2. What animals can be *trained*?
3. What animals are symbols of *power*?
4. What animals are *gentle*?
5. When do you follow *instructions*?
6. Which singer do you think has a good *voice*?

COMPREHENSION

UNDERSTANDING THE READING

Circle the letter of the correct answer.

1. Elephants in Thailand are symbols of _____.

   a. trees and forests   **b.** power and peace   **c.** work and play

2. Elephants work in the _____.

   a. forests   **b.** trucks   **c.** rivers

3. Elephants can _____.

   a. float down the river   **b.** cut down trees   **c.** go up mountains

REMEMBERING DETAILS

*Circle **T** if the sentence is true. Circle **F** if the sentence is false.*

1. Elephants did important work in Thailand.	T	F
2. The men carry the trees to the river.	T	F
3. The elephants trained every day for three hours.	T	F
4. The elephant begins to work at age thirty-five.	T	F
5. A *mahout* trained, fed, and took care of his elephant.	T	F
6. Today, most elephants work with tourists.	T	F

SENTENCE COMPLETION

Match the words in column A and column B to make sentences.

A	B
_____ 1. An elephant understood	**a.** in the forests.
_____ 2. The elephants worked	**b.** strong and gentle.
_____ 3. The elephant is	**c.** and took care of his elephant.
_____ 4. A *mahout* fed	**d.** its *mahout's* instructions.
_____ 5. Elephants trained	**e.** trees to the river.
_____ 6. Elephants carry	**f.** for twenty years.

DICTATION

Work with a partner. Read three sentences from the exercise above. Your partner listens and writes the sentences. Then your partner reads three sentences and you write them.

DISCUSSION

Discuss the answers to these questions with your classmates.

1. Some people think it is bad to make animals work. What do you think?
2. What is your favorite animal? Why?
3. Elephants are intelligent. What other animals are intelligent? How do they help people?

CRITICAL THINKING

Work with a partner. Ask each other the following questions. Discuss your answers.

1. Most people love to see the elephants at the zoo. But lately, many people say it is cruel and selfish to keep elephants in a zoo. Do you agree or disagree with this, and why? Do you think we should have any zoos at all? What are the good points about zoos? What are the bad points?
2. Elephants in Thailand are symbols of power and peace. Name five other animals that are symbolic to people. What does each of them symbolize? What animal are you most like? Why?

WRITING

Complete the sentences about elephants in Thailand.

EXAMPLE   Elephants are a _very important part of Thailand's history_ .

1. Elephants are _____ .

2. Elephants helped _____ .

3. The *mahout* _____ .

4. Elephants worked _____ .

5. Today, most elephants _____ .

SPELLING AND PUNCTUATION

WORDS WITH *PH* THAT SOUND LIKE *F*

> In some words, we spell the *f* sound with *ph.*
> **ph**ysics   ele**ph**ant   paragra**ph**

Underline the misspelled words. Write the correct sentences on the lines.

1. Elefants work in the phorests of Thailand.

   _____

2. Filip is reading about the geografy of Thailand.

   _____

3. Here's a fhoto of my nefew on an elefant.

   _____

4. I will fone my Thai friend to ask about elefants.

   _____

5. This elepant is an orfan. He has no mother or phather.

   _____

 Go to page 141 for the Internet Activity.

| **DID YOU KNOW?** | • There is now a retirement home for sick or old elephants. It will take up to 200 elephants.
• One hundred years ago, there were 100,000 elephants in Thailand. Today there are 4–5,000, with 50% in the wild. | |

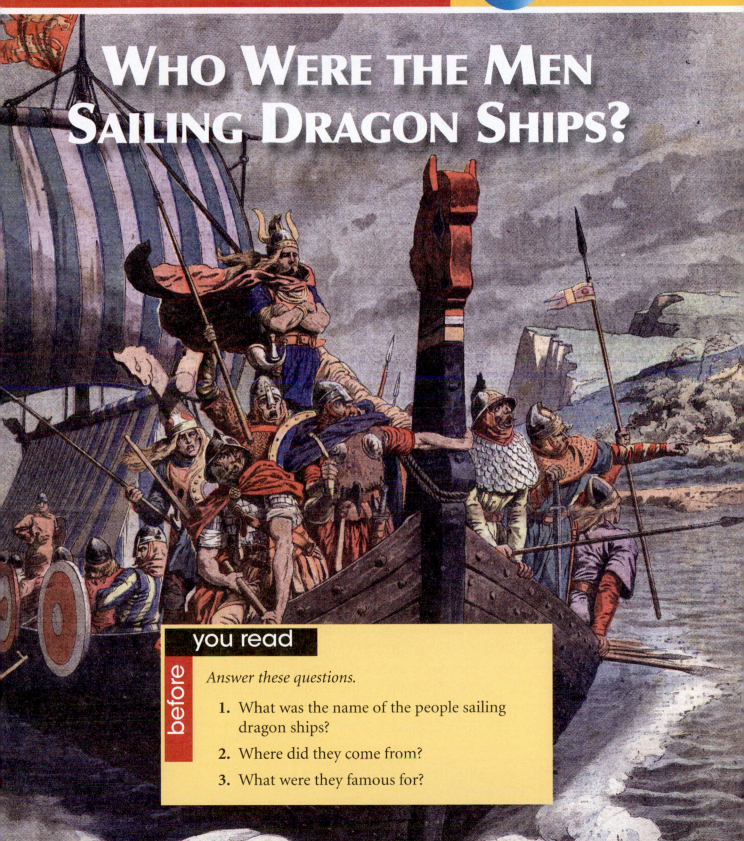

WHO WERE THE MEN SAILING DRAGON SHIPS?

before you read

Answer these questions.

1. What was the name of the people sailing dragon ships?

2. Where did they come from?

3. What were they famous for?

WHO WERE THE MEN SAILING DRAGON SHIPS?

1   They were the Vikings. Around 793, they and their ships started appearing along the coasts of England, France, and other European countries. The Vikings came from northern Europe, from what is now Norway, Sweden, and Denmark. They were a tall, strong people with blue eyes and **fair hair**. In their homeland, most Vikings were farmers. They were also great sailors and shipbuilders. They had the best ships of any people at that time. Their warships were **slim** and fast. They were called *dragon ships* because they had a dragon's head **at the front**. For 200 years, the Vikings used their famous ships to sail to foreign lands.

2   Not all Vikings were the same or wanted the same things from their travels. Some Vikings used their dragon ships to **raid** villages and towns along the coasts and rivers. They wanted to get rich quickly and took what they could. They were **pirates** and **fierce** fighters. Everywhere in Europe, people were afraid of them.

3   Other Vikings were explorers or traders. They used their ships to look for better land or things to trade. They sailed all over Europe and the North Atlantic. When they got to a place they liked, they **settled** there. England was such a place. Iceland was another. And people say the Vikings were the first Russians. The Vikings even sailed as far as North America around the year 1000—almost 500 years before Christopher Columbus!

4   The Vikings were organized and had laws. The word *law* in English is a Viking word. They had regular meetings called *Things*. There they made laws. A man called a *law-speaker* **learned** the laws **by heart**. Then he recited them so that everyone heard and understood them. Every free man and woman had the right to speak there. Men and women generally were equal under the law. At the *Thing*, they punished **criminals** also. The most common **punishment** was a **fine**.

5   When the Vikings settled in a foreign land, they mixed with the **local** people. The local people adopted some Viking words and customs. For example, in English, words like *husband*, *egg*, *knife*, and *window* come from the Viking language. Also, some days of the week are named after Viking gods: Wednesday is Woden's Day, Thursday is Thor's Day, and Friday is Freya's Day. As for Viking customs, *Yule* was an important Viking festival in the middle of winter. People gave gifts and had feasts. Their gods traveled across the sky and brought good things—just like Santa Claus does today at Christmas!

 VOCABULARY

MEANING

Write the correct words in the blanks.

criminals	fine	pirates	raid	slim
fierce	local	punishment	settled	

1. When the Vikings liked a new place, they lived, or _____ there.

2. Their warships were not wide. They were _____.

3. The Vikings had laws. People who did something against the law were

   _____.

4. They gave him a _____ because he did something wrong.

5. They told him he had to pay some money, or a _____.

6. The Vikings were strong and violent. They were _____.

7. Some Vikings were not peaceful. They liked to _____ other people's

   towns and villages.

8. They used their ships to take everything they could from other people. They were

   _____.

9. When they settled somewhere, the Vikings mixed with the _____

   people.

WORDS THAT GO TOGETHER

Write the correct words in the blanks.

at the front	fair hair	learned . . . by heart

1. The law speaker learned the laws so he could remember all of them correctly.

   He _____ them _____.

2. The Vikings, in general, did not have black or brown hair. They had

   _____.

3. _____ of the ship, there was a dragon's head.

USE

Work with a partner to answer the questions. Use complete sentences.

1. What is a *fierce* animal for you?
2. What do most people do to be *slim*?
3. When do people pay a *fine*, for example?
4. Which country has a lot of people with *fair hair*?
5. Who is sitting *at the front of* the class right now?
6. What do you usually *learn by heart*?

COMPREHENSION

UNDERSTANDING THE READING

Circle the letter of the correct answer.

1. The Vikings traveled as _____.

   a. farmers
   b. pirates, explorers, or traders
   c. shipbuilders

2. At a *Thing*, the Vikings got together to _____.

   a. worship their gods
   b. build their ships
   c. make laws

3. When the Vikings settled in a foreign land, they _____.

   a. mixed with the local people
   b. sent away the local people
   c. killed the local people

REMEMBERING DETAILS

Reread the passage and answer the questions.

1. What did the Vikings look like?
2. What were the Viking warships called?
3. When the Vikings traveled, what did they look for?
4. How did European people feel about the Vikings?
5. What was the most common Viking punishment for criminals?
6. When did the Vikings have their *Yule* festival?

SENTENCE COMPLETION

Match the words in column A and column B to make sentences.

	A		B
_____	**1.** The Vikings liked	**a.**	the Vikings.
_____	**2.** They were great	**b.**	in the middle of winter.
_____	**3.** Europeans were afraid of	**c.**	to sail to new places.
_____	**4.** The Vikings had	**d.**	sailors and shipbuilders.
_____	**5.** They had a festival	**e.**	gifts and had feasts.
_____	**6.** People gave	**f.**	laws and punishments.

DICTATION

Work with a partner. Read three sentences from the exercise above. Your partner listens and writes the sentences. Then your partner reads three sentences and you write them.

DISCUSSION

Discuss the answers to these questions with your classmates.

1. Who were the first people to settle in your country? Where did they come from? How did they get there?

2. What did the early people of your country do to survive? Were they farmers, fishermen, or herders? What are your people famous for producing? Did the people of your country settle in other lands? If yes, where did they go?

3. What countries in history were famous for their ships and explorers?

CRITICAL THINKING

Work with a partner. Ask each other the following questions. Discuss your answers.

1. Are there any places left to explore today? Would you like to travel to faraway places where few or no people live? Why or why not? Where would you like to live other than where you live now? Why?

2. A thousand years ago, every free person had a right to speak at the *Thing*. At the *Thing*, the Vikings made laws and punished criminals. What are the good points about this system? What are the bad points? Is this a good system of government for today? Why or why not?

WRITING

Complete the sentences about the Vikings.

EXAMPLE The Vikings came from what is now *Norway, Sweden, and Denmark*   .

1. Viking ships _____.

2. Some Vikings _____.

3. Other Vikings _____.

4. At the *Thing*, _____.

5. In English, some of the days of the week _____.

SPELLING AND PUNCTUATION

DAYS OF THE WEEK: ABBREVIATIONS

The following are **abbreviations** for the **days of the week**. We put a **period after** an abbreviation.

Monday	**Mon.**	Friday	**Fri.**
Tuesday	**Tues.**	Saturday	**Sat.**
Wednesday	**Wed.**	Sunday	**Sun.**
Thursday	**Thurs.**		

Do not forget the abbreviations for the months of the year (see page 80).

Write complete words for these abbreviated dates.

1. Thurs., Aug. 2   _____

2. Sat., Dec. 7   _____

3. Tues., Mar. 15   _____

4. Sun., Sept. 24   _____

5. Wed., Jan. 31   _____

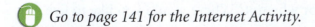 *Go to page 141 for the Internet Activity.*

Go to page 141 for the Internet Activity.

DID YOU KNOW?	• The English complained that the Vikings combed their hair too much and were too clean. Vikings bathed once a week! • Viking men wore make-up to make themselves more handsome.	

HOW DID THE RED CROSS START?

HOW DID THE RED CROSS START?

1   In 1859, a Swiss man named Henry Dunant went to Italy **on business**. At the time, there was a war in Italy. The French and the Italian armies were fighting the Austrian army. On the evening of June 24, 1859, Dunant arrived in the town of Solferino. He got there just after a big battle near the town that day. There were thousands of **wounded** soldiers left on the battlefield.[1] But nobody was there to take care of them. Dunant was **shocked**.

2   Dunant asked the people of the town to help the wounded soldiers. He organized the work of the **volunteers**. Later, he wrote a book called *A Memory of Solferino*. In it, he described what happened after that battle. He also talked about what to do in future wars to help wounded soldiers. One of his ideas was that every country should have an organization of trained volunteers to take care of the wounded. Another one of his ideas was that there should be international treaties[2] to protect these volunteers.

3   In 1863, Dunant and four other Swiss men **founded** the International Committee of the Red Cross. A year later, in 1864, the Red Cross organized an international conference in Geneva, Switzerland. There, twelve countries **signed** the first Geneva Convention. This international treaty established rules for the protection of wounded soldiers, medical personnel, and volunteers in a war. It also introduced a protection **symbol** for medical personnel and volunteers: a red cross on a white background.

4   **By now**, Dunant was famous as the founder of the Red Cross. He was busy helping it grow all over the world. But there was one problem: He didn't have time for his own business. His business was **losing money**. Dunant had to **resign** from the Red Cross. After that, and for many years, he was forgotten. It is only in 1895 that a **journalist** rediscovered Dunant and wrote about him. Dunant became famous again. Finally, in 1901, he won the first Nobel Peace Prize for founding the Red Cross.

5   The symbol of the Red Cross is a red cross on a white background. It is the **reverse** of the flag of Switzerland. Muslim countries use a red crescent instead of a cross. A crescent looks like a half-moon. Today, 186 countries are part of the International Red Cross and Red Crescent movement. When there is a war or a disaster anywhere in the world, Red Cross or Red Crescent volunteers take care of the wounded and other victims. It all started 150 years ago on the battlefield of Solferino with one extraordinary man, Henry Dunant.

---

[1] **battlefield**: a place where soldiers fight a battle
[2] **treaty**: a written agreement between two or more countries

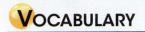

VOCABULARY

MEANING

Write the correct words in the blanks.

founded	resign	shocked	symbol	wounded
journalist	reverse	signed	volunteers	

1. He writes stories for newspapers and magazines. He is a _____.

2. Many soldiers were _____. They were badly hurt.

3. People took care of the wounded men. They did not get paid for this. They were _____.

4. People from twelve countries _____ a treaty. They wrote their names on the treaty.

5. Dunant had to stop working at the Red Cross. He had to _____.

6. A red cross on a white background is the _____ of the Red Cross. It is the Red Cross's sign.

7. Dunant was very surprised and upset. He was _____.

8. The Swiss flag has a white cross on a red background. The Red Cross flag has a red cross on a white background. The Red Cross flag is the _____ of the Swiss flag.

9. Dunant and four other Swiss men _____, or started the International Committee of the Red Cross.

WORDS THAT GO TOGETHER

Write the correct words in the blanks.

by now	losing money	on business

1. Dunant did not go to the town of Solferino for a vacation. He went there _____.

2. Dunant had a lot of money before and up until this time. He was rich _____.

3. Dunant's business had problems. The business was _____.

USE

Work with a partner to answer these questions. Use complete sentences.

1. What *shocks* you?
2. Who is a famous *journalist*?
3. How do *volunteers* help people?
4. What is something you *sign*?
5. What is something people do *on business*?
6. Why does a person usually *resign* from a job?

COMPREHENSION

UNDERSTANDING THE READING

Circle the letter of the correct answer.

1. Dunant asked the people of Solferino to _____.

   a. help wounded soldiers
   b. end the war
   c. join the Red Cross

2. Henry Dunant _____.

   a. always worked for the Red Cross
   b. was always famous
   c. won the first Nobel Peace Prize

3. The symbol of the Red Cross is _____.

   a. different in every country
   b. the same in every country
   c. a red cross

REMEMBERING DETAILS

Reread the passage and answer the questions.

1. What country did Henry Dunant go to in 1859?
2. What shocked Dunant?
3. What were Dunant's ideas?
4. What conference did he help organize?
5. How did he become famous again?
6. How many countries are part of the Red Cross and Red Crescent movement today?

UNDERSTANDING THE SEQUENCE

Which happened first? Write 1 on the line. Which happened second? Write 2 on the line.

1. _____ Dunant wrote a book.

   _____ Dunant was shocked by what he saw on the battlefield of Solferino.

2. _____ Dunant and four other men founded the Red Cross.

   _____ Twelve countries signed the first Geneva Convention.

3. _____ Dunant's business lost a lot of money.

   _____ Dunant resigned from the International Committee of the Red Cross

4. _____ Dunant won the first Nobel Peace Prize.

   _____ A journalist wrote about Dunant.

TELL THE STORY

Work with a partner. Tell the story of Henry Dunant to your partner. Use your own words. Your partner asks you questions about the story. Then your partner tells you the story and you ask questions.

DISCUSSION

Discuss the answers to these questions with your classmates.

1. The Red Cross is an international aid organization. They help people all over the world. What other international aid organizations do you know? What do they do?
2. Is it better to give money to an aid organization or to do volunteer work?
3. Do you want to belong to an aid organization? How do you want to help people?

CRITICAL THINKING

Work with a partner. Ask each other the following questions. Discuss your answers.

1. How does the story of Henry Dunant make you feel? Why? What character and personality traits do you think Dunant had? Why does it take so long sometimes for the world to recognize the good that a person has done?
2. What do you think about volunteer and aid organizations around the world? Are they good or bad? Does your country have a Red Cross or Red Crescent society? How have they helped people? Do people in your country do a lot of volunteer work? Why or why not?

WRITING

Complete the sentences about the Red Cross.

EXAMPLE   The Red Cross started *in Switzerland* _____.

1. Henry Dunant went _____.

2. Henry Dunant had ideas _____.

3. Henry Dunant and four other Swiss men _____.

4. Henry Dunant helped organize _____.

5. Today, there are _____.

SPELLING AND PUNCTUATION

CAPITAL LETTERS: ORGANIZATIONS AND RELIGIONS

> We use a **capital letter** for the **main words** in the name of an **organization**.
> We do NOT use a capital letter for *the* or *of* in the name.
>   *Henry Dunant founded the International Committee of the Red Cross.*
>
> We use a **capital letter** for the names of **religions** and their **followers**.
>   *The crescent is a symbol of Islam.*
>   *Many Muslims help the poor in different countries.*

Underline the words that need capital letters. Circle the words with incorrect capital letters. Correct all these words.

1. The Symbol of the red cross is a red cross on a white background.

2. The red crescent has offices in muslim countries.

3. Another Organization that helps people is doctors without borders.

4. There are a lot of roman catholics in Switzerland.

5. The protestants are the second largest religious group in Switzerland.

 Go to page 141 for the Internet Activity.

Go to page 141 for the Internet Activity.

| **DID YOU KNOW?** | • The Red Cross/Crescent is the largest volunteer organization in the United States and in the world.
• More than 1.2 million people volunteer with the Red Cross in the U.S. | |

A. COMPREHENSION

Circle the letter of the correct answer.

1. Andrew Carnegie was a rich man who _____.
   a. was only interested in making himself richer
   b. used all of his money to build railroads
   c. didn't believe schools were important for success
   d. gave most of his money for education and peace

2. Antarctica _____.
   a. has only a few cities
   b. has no plants or land animals
   c. is a nice place to live in the summer
   d. looks a lot like the Sahara Desert

3. In the past, some people lived under the ground because _____.
   a. there was no room for more homes above the ground
   b. they didn't like sunlight and open spaces
   c. they wanted protection
   d. they wanted to do something unusual

4. Most people decorate their bodies because they want to _____.
   a. look more attractive
   b. protect their skin
   c. look healthy
   d. be different from everyone else

5. The Uros _____.
   a. travel from one place to another around Peru
   b. no longer live in their traditional ways
   c. use a reed plant for shelter, food, and medicine
   d. refuse to accept any modern ways of life

6. In ice hockey, players _____.

   a. use a stick to hit a puck across the ice to the other team's goal

   b. use their skates to kick a puck across the ice into the other team's goal

   c. try to get a puck that is on the other side of the ice by skating faster than the other team

   d. throw a puck across the ice to the other team's goal

7. New Zealand _____.

   a. has a large number of people living in a small amount of space

   b. is an isolated country with a low population and large areas of natural beauty

   c. is famous for its spectacular cities, monuments, and ancient civilizations

   d. is populated mostly by native people living in traditional ways

8. In the past in Thailand, a *mahout* trained his elephant to _____.

   a. give rides to tourists on its back

   b. carry trees from the forest

   c. fight with him in battles

   d. take care of his children

9. The Viking explorers _____.

   a. wanted to conquer and destroy the new places they discovered

   b. stayed mostly in Northern Europe during their travels

   c. didn't bring their ways of life to the places they discovered

   d. settled among the people they found and shared their customs

10. The purpose of the Red Cross is to _____.

   a. bring countries together for a common purpose

   b. stop wars around the world

   c. protect wounded soldiers

   d. help the people of poor countries

B. VOCABULARY

Complete the definitions. Circle the letter of the correct answer.

1. You do something immediately. You do it _____.
    a. as much   b. right away   c. by now   d. nearly
       as possible

2. Something very, very big is _____.
    a. dangerous   b. normal   c. attractive   d. huge

3. You want to make a hole in the ground. You _____ in the ground.
    a. cover   b. drop   c. dig   d. decide

4. You pull something to make it bigger. You _____ it.
    a. stretch   b. spread   c. return   d. train

5. Traditional things made by hand are _____.
    a. ties   b. tribes   c. rafts   d. handicrafts

6. One thing is like another thing. It is _____ it.
    a. similar to   b. made of   c. side by side   d. belongs to

7. A place far away from other places and difficult to reach is _____.
    a. isolated   b. spectacular   c. civilized   d. crowded

8. You follow rules or orders. You follow _____.
    a. teams   b. instructions   c. purposes   d. supplies

9. When the punishment is paying money, it is a _____.
    a. criminal   b. good   c. fine   d. fan

10. People are hurt in a fight or war. They are _____.
    a. dangerous   b. wrapped   c. wounded   d. shocked

C. SPELLING AND PUNCTUATION

Circle the letter of the sentence with the correct spelling and punctuation.

1. **a.** Andrew Carnegie gave away over $350 millions.

    b. Andrew Carnegie gave away over $350s million.

    c. Andrew Carnegie gave away over $350 million.

    d. Andrew Carnegie gave away over $350 Million.

2. **a.** Ships go to Antarctica during the Summer months from November to February.

    b. Ships go to antarctica during the summer months from november to february.

    c. Ships go to Antarctica during the summer months from November to February.

    d. Ships go to Antarctica during the summer months from November to february.

3. **a.** Coober Pedy is in Australia!

    b. Thousands of people live underground!

    c. Where is Australia!

    d. The native people are called Aboriginal peopl

4. **a.** People get tattooss to show they belong to a group.

    b. People get tattoos to show they belong to a group.

    c. People get tattooes to show they belong to a group.

    d. People get Tattoos to show they belong to a group.

5. **a.** The Uros live on lake Titicaca in South America.

    b. The Uros live on Lake Titicaca in South America.

    c. The Uros live on Lake Titicaca in south America.

    d. The Uros live on lake titicaca in South America.

6. **a.** Canadas favorite sport is ice hockey.

    b. Canadas' favorite sport is ice hockey.

    c. Canada favorite sport is ice hockey.

    d. Canada's favorite sport is ice hockey.

7. **a.** The movie *The chronicles of narnia* was filmed in New Zealand.

  b. The movie *The Chronicles Of Narnia* was filmed in New Zealand.

  c. The movie *The Chronicles of Narnia* was filmed in New Zealand.

  d. The movie *the chronicles of Narnia* was filmed in New Zealand.

8. **a.** This biography of a *mahout* is phantastic!

  b. This biografhy of a *mahout* is fantastic!

  c. This biografy of a *mahout* is fantastic!

  d. This biography of a *mahout* is fantastic!

9. **a.** I'm here on Tues., Thurs., Fr., and Sat.

  b. I'm here on Tues., Thurs., Fri., and Sat.

  c. I'm here on Tu., Thurs., Fri., and Sat.

  d. I'm here on Tue., Thur., Fri., and Sat.

10. **a.** The Red Cross is the Red Crescent in muslim countries.

  b. the red cross is the red crescent in Muslim countries.

  c. The Red Cross is the Red Crescent in Muslim countries.

  d. The Red cross is The Red crescent in Muslim countries.

APPENDICES

INTERNET ACTIVITIES

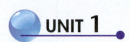 **UNIT 1**

J.R.R. Tolkien wrote three books called *The Lord of the Rings*. Like the *Harry Potter* books, both young people and adults loved *The Lord of the Rings*. They also became movies.

Work in a small group. Use the Internet to find information about J.R.R. Tolkien and The Lord of the Rings. *Answer the questions. Share your information with your classmates.*

1. Where and when was J.R.R. Tolkien born?
2. In what country did he live most of his life?
3. When did Tolkien write *The Lord of the Rings*?
4. In general, what is *The Lord of the Rings* about?
5. What other books did Tolkien write? (Name two)

 **UNIT 2**

Work in a small group. Use the Internet to find information on New Year customs around the world. Choose one country from the list and answer the questions. Share your information with your classmates.

Belgium	Egypt	Germany	Thailand
China	Ethiopia	Iran	Vietnam

1. How do the people of this country celebrate the New Year?
2. Do they have special customs, eat special foods, or wear certain clothing?
3. What is the meaning of each custom?

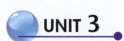 **UNIT 3**

Work in a small group. Use the Internet to find out about the White House (where the president of the United States lives). Answer the questions. Share your information with your classmates.

1. Where and when was the White House built?
2. How many floors does the White House have?
3. Where do the President and his family live?
4. Where do the President and the First Lady work?
5. What is the President's official schedule for one day? Choose the day you want.

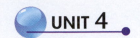

UNIT 4

Work in a small group. Use the Internet to find two animals that are sacred in the following countries or cultures: Ancient Egypt, Japan, China, Bali, Native Americans. Share your information with your classmates.

COUNTRY/CULTURE	SACRED ANIMALS
ANCIENT EGYPT	1.
	2.
JAPAN	1.
	2.
CHINA	1.
	2.
BALI	1.
	2.
NATIVE AMERICANS	1.
	2.

UNIT 5

Work in a small group. Use the Internet to learn more about wedding gift-giving customs around the world. Answer the questions. Share your information with your classmates.

1. What does a groom in Sudan give to the bride's family? Why?
2. What does a groom in Fiji present to the bride's father?
3. In China, what does the groom's family give to the bride's family on the day they are betrothed?
4. What is "bride price" in India? Why is it controversial today?
5. What does a groom give his bride in the Philippines?
6. Which websites have the best information?

UNIT 6

Work in a small group. Use the Internet to learn more about blowfish. Answer the questions. Share your information with your classmates.

1. What does a blowfish look like?
2. Where in the ocean do blowfish live?
3. What do they eat?
4. What happens if a larger fish eats a blowfish?
5. How did the ancient Egyptians use the blowfish?
6. How do fishermen catch blowfish?
7. Why are the blowfish in danger today?
8. Which websites have the best information?
9. Which have the best pictures?

UNIT 7

Work in a small group. Use the Internet to learn about the Inuit. Answer the questions. Share your information with your classmates.

1. Who are the Inuit?
2. Where do they live?
3. What is the geography and climate of these places?
4. What do traditional Inuit homes look like?
5. What do their houses look like now?
6. What kinds of work do the Inuit do?
7. What is their traditional clothing made from?
8. What do they eat and drink?
9. How do they travel?
10. Do they have their own language?

UNIT 8

Work in a small group. Use the Internet to learn about oceans. Answer the questions. Share your information with your classmates.

1. Why are oceans important? Give two reasons.
2. How are humans polluting the oceans? Give two causes of pollution.
3. What can people do to save the oceans? Give two possible ways of saving the oceans.
4. Which websites have the most information?

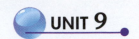 **UNIT 9**

Work in a small group. Look at the list of great monuments or "wonders" of the world. Use the Internet to research ONE of them. Answer the questions. Share your information with your classmates.

Angkor Wat	the Great Pyramid of Giza	Stonehenge
Chichen Itza	the Parthenon	the Taj Mahal

1. When and where was it built?
2. Who built it?
3. What is it? (Give a short description.)
4. Which websites have the best information?

 **UNIT 10**

Work in a small group. Use the Internet to find a survival story (a story of someone who lived through a dangerous storm or natural disaster like a tornado, earthquake, tsunami, flood, etc.). Share the story with your classmates.

 **UNIT 11**

Work in a small group. Look at the list of rich people, past and present. Use the Internet to research ONE of them. Answer the questions. Share your information with your classmates.

Bill Gates	Li Ka-shing	John D. Rockefeller
Hetty Green	Aristotle Onassis	Oprah Winfrey

1. When was he or she born?
2. Where did he or she live? OR Where does he or she live?
3. How did he or she get rich?
4. What did he or she do with his or her money? OR What does he or she do with his or her money?
5. Which websites have the best information?

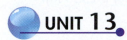

UNIT 12

Work in a small group. Look at the list of places where living conditions are extremely difficult. Use the Internet to research ONE of them. Answer the questions. Share your information with your classmates.

the Amazon rain forest	the Gobi Desert	the Sahara Desert
Death Valley	the North Pole	Siberia

1. Where is it located?
2. What is the weather like?
3. What are the highest and lowest temperatures in that place?
4. What does the place look like?
5. Why is it difficult to live there?

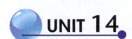

UNIT 13

Work in a small group. Look at the list of some unusual houses and buildings. Use the Internet to research ONE of them. Answer the questions. Share your information with your classmates.

the Basket Building	the Crooked House	the Kettle House
the Bubble House	the Dancing House	the Mushroom House
the Crazy House	the Football House	the Thin House

1. Where is it located?
2. When was it built?
3. Who built it?
4. What is unusual about this house or building?

UNIT 14

Work in a small group. Use the Internet to look up the traditional tattoos of the Maori people. Find pictures of Maori men and women with tattoos, and answer the questions. Share the pictures and your information with your classmates.

1. What is the name for their tattoos?
2. How do they make them?
3. What are they used for?
4. What do they mean?
5. Who wears them?
6. Which websites have the best information? Which have the best pictures?

UNIT 15

Work in a small group. Look at the list of disappearing cultures. Use the Internet to research ONE of them. Answer the questions. Share your information with your classmates.

Aborigines	Chipaya	San (Bushmen)
Ariaal	Penan	Tarahumara

1. Where do these people live?
2. Why is their culture disappearing?
3. Which websites have the best information?

UNIT 16

Work in a small group. Look at the list of sports. Use the Internet to research ONE of them. Find out where, when, and how it began. Share your information with your classmates.

basketball	curling	golf	rugby
camel racing	dog sledding	polo	skiing

UNIT 17

Work in a small group. Imagine that you have five days to visit New Zealand. Use the Internet to find a travel guide to New Zealand. Write a travel schedule that tells where you want to go and what you want to do and see in those five days. You can see and do more than one thing in a day. Share your schedule with your classmates.

Day 1	Day 2	Day 3	Day 4	Day 5
• Visit the Auckland Museum				

UNIT 18

Work in a small group. Look at the list of animals that help people. Use the Internet to research ONE of them. Answer the questions. Share your information with your classmates.

Alaskan husky	camel	mule	ox
bloodhound	llama	New Zealand huntaway	red-tailed hawk

1. What does the animal look like?
2. How does the animal help people?
3. In what areas or countries is this animal often used?

UNIT 19

Work in a small group. Use the Internet to learn more about the Vikings. Answer the questions. Share your information with your classmates.

1. What are the dates of the Viking Age?
2. What kind of clothes did the Vikings wear?
3. What kind of houses did they live in?
4. What did they make their ships from?
5. What kind of weapons did they have?
6. In what areas did they settle?
7. Which websites have the best information? Which have the best pictures?

UNIT 20

Work in a small group. Look at the list of aid organizations. Use the Internet to research ONE of them. Answer the questions. Share your information with your classmates.

Doctors Without Borders	the Salvation Army
OXFAM	UNICEF

1. Who founded the organization?
2. When and where?
3. What does the organization do?

MAP OF THE WORLD

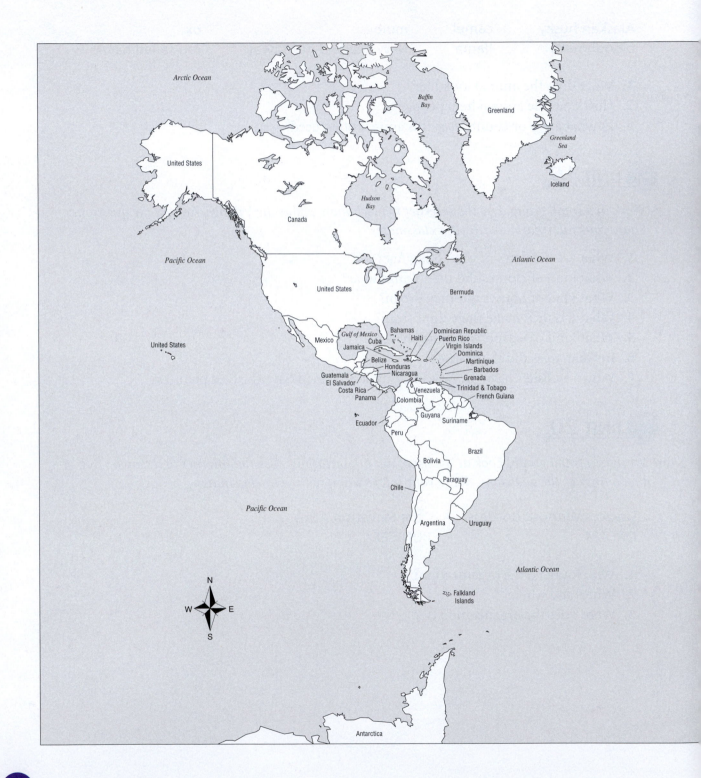

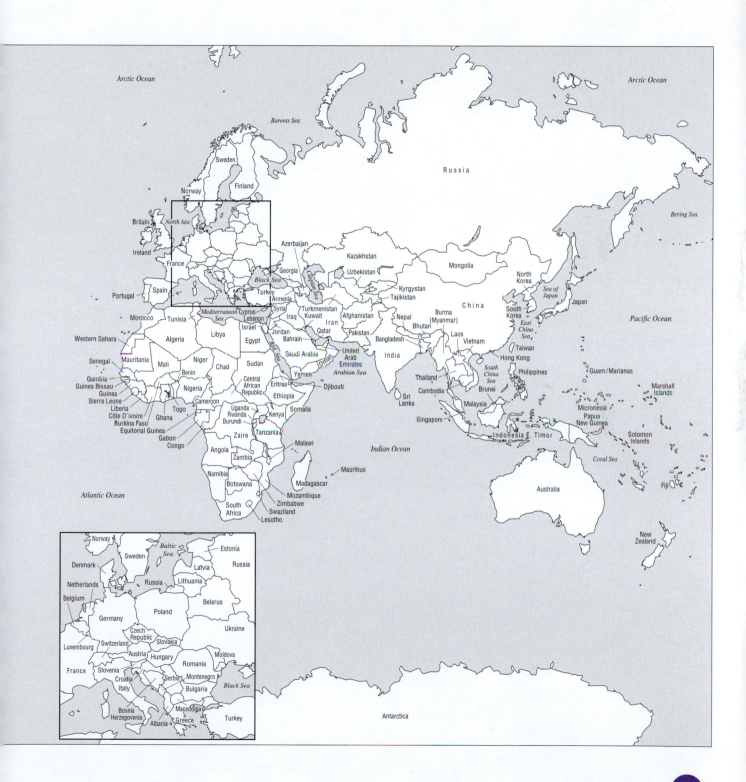

Arctic Ocean

Arctic Ocean

Barents Sea

Bering Sea

Sweden

Norway

Finland

R u s s i a

Britain

North Sea

Azerbaijan

Kazakhstan

Mongolia

North
Korea

Sea of
Japan

Ireland

France

Georgia

Black Sea

Caspian Sea

Uzbekistan

Kyrgystan

C h i n a

South
Korea

Japan

Pacific Ocean

Portugal

Spain

Turkey

Armenia

Turkmenistan

Tajikistan

Burma
(Myanmar)

East
China
Sea

Mediterranean
Sea

Cyprus

Syria

Iraq

Kuwait

Iran

Afghanistan

Nepal

Bhutan

Laos

Vietnam

Taiwan

Morocco

Tunisia

Lebanon

Israel

Jordan

Bahrain

Qatar

Pakistan

Bangladesh

Hong Kong

Western Sahara

Algeria

Libya

Egypt

Saudi Arabia

United
Arab
Emirates

India

South
China
Sea

Philippines

Guam/Marianas

Senegal

Mauritania

Mali

Niger

Chad

Sudan

Oman

Yemen

Arabian Sea

Thailand

Brunei

Marshall
Islands

Gambia

Guinea Bissau

Benin

Central
African
Republic

Eritrea

Djibouti

Sri
Lanka

Cambodia

Malaysia

Micronesia

Guinea

Nigeria

Ethiopia

Papua
New Guinea

Sierra Leone

Liberia

Côte D'ivoire

Ghana

Cameroon

Uganda

Rwanda

Somalia

Singapore

Indonesia

E. Timor

Solomon
Islands

Burkina Faso

Togo

Kenya

Equitorial Guinea

Gabon

Congo

Zaire

Burundi

Tanzania

Angola

Malawi

Indian Ocean

Coral Sea

Fiji

Zambia

Mauritius

Namibia

Botswana

Madagascar

Australia

Atlantic Ocean

South
Africa

Mozambique

Zimbabwe

Swaziland

New
Zealand

Lesotho

Antarctica

Norway

Baltic
Sea

Estonia

Russia

Denmark

Sweden

Latvia

Netherlands

Russia

Lithuania

Belgium

Poland

Belarus

Germany

Ukraine

Luxembourg

Czech
Republic

Slovakia

France

Switzerland

Austria

Hungary

Moldova

Slovenia

Romania

Croatia

Serbia

Montenegro

Italy

Bulgaria

Black Sea

Bosnia
Herzegovenia

Macedonia

Albania

Greece

Turkey